How to Organise My Office

Published by
Lotus Press

How to Organise My Office

Philip J. Samuel

Lotus PRESS
4263/3, Ansari Road,
Darya Ganj, New Delhi-110002

Lotus Press
4263/3, Ansari Road, Darya Ganj, New Delhi- 110002
Ph.: 32903912, 23280047, E-mail: lotus_press@sify.com
www.lotuspress.co.in

HOW TO ORGANISE MY OFFICE

ISBN: 81-8382-019-0

Reprint : 2006, 2007, 2008

Published by: Lotus Press, New Delhi-110 002.
Laser Typeset by: Reliable Infomedia, N. Delhi-9
Printed at: Nisha Enterprises, Delhi.

PREFACE

In today's turbo-charged work environment, excellent organisation can mean the difference between seizing a career opportunity and watching it fly by. A well-organised office also means efficient invoicing, expensing and follow-up, which translates into dollars in your pocket—or out the window. For home-based businesses, organisation is doubly important. A good system can help set boundaries between home life and work life, giving more time to actually enjoy the freedom of being your own boss.

Whether you are just setting up a small or home office or just frustrated with how all the clutter in your office space is interfering with your productivity, this book will show you how to get your office organised and turn your office space into a workspace. It contains simple routines for managing your office in easy step-by-step methods. The topics covered in this book include: how to manage your office effectively, how to setup your office, how to select the right facility, how to equip your office, how to keep security and safety in your office etc. It also provides a mixture of common-sense suggestions and useful organisational tips.

Editor

In today's turbo-charged work environment, excellent organisation can mean the difference between seizing a career opportunity and watching it fly by. A well-organised office also means efficient invoicing, expensing and follow-up, which translates into dollars in your pocket—or out the window.

This book contains simple routines for managing your office in easy step-by-step methods. The topics covered in this book include: how to manage your office effectively, how to setup your office, how to select the right facility, how to equip your office, how to keep security and safety in your office etc. It also provides a mixture of common-sense sugge-stions and useful organisational tips.

CONTENTS

1

HOW TO DESIGN MY OFFICE

Commercial office facilities were originally designed to be office spaces; they have adequate power, lighting and ventilation for office work spaces built into their design. This will probably not be the case with your house or other building that you've decided to use as a small or home office. Each of the home office design elements and the infrastructure needs for home office use are described below.

1.1. POWER

Commercial buildings designed for office use generally have a better quality electrical supply than residences and other non-commercial buildings. And setting up a small or home office means that you will be greatly increasing your power use in that location. For instance, even a small laser printer will consume 300 to 400 watts of electricity when it's running, and larger laser printers will consume much more. Now think of the other office equipment you're about to install in your home office. Suppose you have a PC, a monitor, a laser printer, a fax machine, a scanner and a phone. Will the circuitry in your chosen home office location be up to the job?

Step one of home office design is assessing your power needs. Add up the wattage of your office equipment (and related office design features such as lighting). You may be able to cut down on your power needs by "combining" some of your office equipment needs. For example, instead of having a separate printer, fax, copier and scanner, you could have one multi-function machine that performed all these functions.

Before you even spare a passing thought to the aesthetics of your home office design, plug in all your equipment and try to use it, as you would on a normal working day. If you experience electrical danger signs, such as breakers popping or lights dimming when various pieces of equipment are operating, have an electrician check your circuitry and see if any simple rewiring can be done.

1.2. LIGHTING

Chances are extremely high that the existing lighting in the proposed location of your small or home office is inadequate for work space needs. Few residences have rows of fluorescent lights installed, for example, as commercial office spaces do. While you don't need to go that far, you do need to incorporate strong overhead lighting in your home office design—and in many cases, that means purchasing and installing new or additional light fixtures. Various types of track lighting are easy to find and relatively easy to install. When choosing the lighting for your home office, assess your needs first by sitting in your proposed work space and determining how much illumination you need to work efficiently and where the light should be placed.

An office with inadequate lighting is not only useless but can lead to all kinds of health problems from headaches through neck and shoulder pain. Remember, though, that adding lighting will increase your office's power loads. Once again, you'll need to be sure your existing circuitry can handle the increased electrical load.

1.3. VENTILATION

Many people overlook the importance of ventilation in office design, but you and your office equipment both need it. First, the more office equipment you have operating, the more heat will be generated—and excessive heat can damage office equipment such as PCs. Secondly, if your small or home office space isn't adequately ventilated, working there can be extremely uncomfortable for you. This is a particularly common problem when people choose small spaces for their home offices, such as ex-bedrooms. The room becomes a "hot box" and almost impossible to work in. Consider the ventilation aspect of your office design carefully when you're choosing the spot for your small or home office.

Is the room large enough for you and your equipment to work in comfortably? Consider cooling options such as purchasing a small air-conditioning unit or fans of an adequate size to cool the room. Commercial office spaces usually have air-conditioning systems installed to protect both the equipment and people's health. Now that you've examined the basic infrastructure of your small or home office design, it's time to give some thought to the utility and safety aspects of your work space.

You've chosen the best location for your small or home office based on your power, lighting and ventilation needs. Now you're ready to set up your home office and see how well your office design meets your work needs. Use this check list to ensure that your small or home office is a safe, usable work space:

Place your office equipment for maximum ease of use: Determine the best place for each piece of office equipment and furniture by running through a work test. Whatever you use frequently should be close to hand and easy to access. If it's not, move it. For instance, if your work involves using the phone a lot, your phone should be in a position where you don't have to get up or reach awkwardly to use it. If your work involves handling and filing a lot of paper, your filing cabinet needs to be close enough that you can get to it with a few steps—or even better, have filing drawers within your desk that are close to hand. Run this work test for several days to be sure you have everything placed in the best position.

Protect your sensitive office equipment: It's equally important to protect your office equipment, such as computers, from power surges and/or electrical outages. Invest in as many UPSs (Uninterrupted Power Supplies) as necessary to prevent loss of data or worse, expensive damage to your equipment.

Organise those cords and wires: Just because you have a lot of office equipment doesn't mean your work space has to look like a rattlesnake den. Plan your office design to put as much of your telephone wire or CAT5 cable out of sight as possible. If you have long lengths of cable running from room to room (or down a hallway), consider drilling holes and lifting baseboards as necessary to get it out of sight. If you can't put cables and/or wires out of harm's way, make sure you tape or staple them down as necessary, close to walls, so people aren't in danger of tripping over them.

Examine the cords of your office equipment and take up the slack where possible, either using wire ties to tie up the excess, or using something like a Cable Turtle. Neatly bundled cords help prevent accidents and will make your home office more aesthetically pleasing. Going wireless is another way of tackling the cords and wires problem that you may want to consider. Many computer peripherals, such as printers and copiers, now have wireless capabilities.

Clear the paths: Because they're situated in rooms that were originally designed for other uses, some small or home offices resemble obstacle courses. Just because that bed or plant stand has always been there, doesn't mean it has to stay there. You need to be able to get up from your desk and walk around without banging your shins. Get rid of all unnecessary furniture and clutter in your home office space. And don't forget to check the floor. Make sure all area rugs are securely tacked down, for instance.

Do a last check of your work needs and make sure that you have all the office equipment and office furniture that you need to keep you organised and able to work productively and safely: For example, a speaker phone will allow you to speak on the phone hands-free, allowing you to make notes or work on other tasks. If you have manuals or books that you consult frequently, incorporating some built-in shelving into your home office design may be a real productivity booster.

Add some eye candy: A well-placed painting or print or even a corkboard with some photos can add some visual punch to your home office design and make your office a more appealing space to work in. Your personal taste will determine what works best for you, but don't clutter up your work space with too many visual distractions. Infrastructure, utility and safety—the keys to office design that will help you create a small or home office that's both a functional work space and a pleasant, productive place to work. Even if we sometimes have little choice as to where our office space will be, focusing on these three elements will help us design an office space that's usable and ultimately livable.

1.4. FUNCTIONALITY

The most important feature of good office design is

functionality. But too often our offices are crammed with so many office machines, equipment, supplies and pieces of paper that our small or home offices are completely dysfunctional. Do you have to move things out of the way before you can sit down and work? Are there so many papers on your desk that they're spilling onto the floor? Do you need to contact a search and rescue team to find whatever it is you're looking for?

Then it's definitely time to roll up your sleeves and organise your office. You can have the most attractive, up-to-date office design available and still not be able to accomplish what you need to do unless you organise your office. These steps for an office makeover will show you how to organise your desk and your office space so that you have an office design you can both appreciate and work in.

1. *Clear the pathways*: A friend had a coffee table in the middle of his office which made moving from the desk to the filing cabinet a shin-cracking task for anyone without the agility and balance of a trained acrobat. As he never entertained clients in his office, the coffee table was only used when he set things on it. Moving the coffee table out gave him a clear walkway and saved him a lot of potential shin damage! Are there furniture obstacles in your office design? Move them or move them out entirely. You need to be able to walk around.

2. *Clear your desktop*: There now. Doesn't that look nice? An office design showpiece! Now the hard part. Begin to organise your office by looking at your office desk and decide what has to be there. Your computer, obviously. Put it back. Your phone, definitely. Put it back, too. But what else? Look at all the other stuff you've taken off your desk and ask yourself, "Does it have to be on my office desk?" If it's not something that you use every day

to make your work easier, it doesn't and it's time to find another place for it. The stack of papers you've been meaning to deal with? Deal with them and file them. The half eaten doughnut from last week.

3. *Get and use caddys and trays to organise your desk and your drawers*: Office supply stores and chain retailers have all kinds of plastic trays and caddies, including those that are designed to fit perfectly into a desk drawer. Use them to get your office supplies organised. Now all those loose pens, paper clips and thumb tacks have a place to go – and when you want one, you'll be able to find it. To further organise your desk, stacking trays are ideal for your "inbox" and "outbox". They'll help you keep your office desktop neat and save space.

4. *Update your equipment*: What office machines are slowing you down or cluttering up your office design? Does your computer need a memory or hard drive upgrade? Maybe it's time to get rid of your old printer, fax machine and scanner and invest in a multi-function printer. Or time to upgrade the primitive touch tone phone to a speaker phone. Increase the functionality of your office design and make some more work space available.

5. *Get it off your desk*: Clear even more work space and organise your office by giving some of your office essentials their own separate space. For instance, your printer or multi-function copier shouldn't be on your desk. Investing in a printer stand will keep it within a usable distance, free more of that valuable desk real estate, and give you some more shelf storage space for accessories such as printer paper. Have a small desk and need even more room? An occasional table placed next to your desk

will add an elegant touch to your office design and serve as an additional working area. Is your desk cluttered with books or manuals? Invest in a book shelf, either freestanding or built-in. You'll be amazed at how much more space you have to work in when you just move a few books off your desk.

6. *Give your eyes something attractive to rest on*: Sit in front of your computer with your hands on the keyboard and look away from the monitor, sweeping 90 degrees. Looking away from the computer screen every few minutes and focusing your eyes on more distant objects to help combat eye strain and fatigue. But is there anything attractive in your range of vision? If not, add something worth looking at to your office design, such as a painting, print or poster that you like. If space allows and the conditions are right, a living blooming plant can work wonders for dressing up an office space and feeding your spirits.
7. *Give your revamped office desk the reach test*: Sit at your new and improved desk and work. Is everything you need within easy reach? Adjust your office design as necessary, moving the items or equipment you need the most into easy reach. You should not have to get up and leave your desk to staple something, for example. Take note of what you don't use, too. If you don't use it much, the organise your office rule is that it should be stored further away.
8. *Check your storage needs*: Small and home offices seem to produce more paper than anything else. And a lot of the stuff that clutters our offices is just stuff that's sitting out because there's no where else to put it. Organise your office by getting another filing cabinet if you need it or adding a supplies cupboard. Then you'll have a place to put it and

keeping your office design uncluttered will be easier.

9. *Set up a recycling centre*: Paper, cardboard, glass, plastic bottles and drink containers – so much of the material that we throw away in our offices is recyclable. Make it easy for people to do the right thing and get the clutter out of your office by setting up a small recycling centre with labelled bins, either in or close to your office. Plastic totes are inexpensive and easy for one person to carry when it comes time to take the recycling to the curb or recycling depot.
10. *Revamp the window treatment*: If your small or home office has windows, remember that the window treatments are part of your office design. A new type and/or colour of blinds or drapes can make a striking visual difference to the atmosphere of your office. Like what you have or don't want to spend the money on updating your window treatments right now? Then opt for a cleaning. Nothing says spring like clean and fresh.
11. *Realign your office desk*: Just because you've used one office design for years doesn't mean you can't change it. Take a critical look at how your office desk is positioned within the room. Moving your desk can give you a whole new perspective and even make you more productive. If your office desk is jammed into a corner, for example, and space allows, pull it out into the middle of the room. If your desk is facing away from the only window, move it closer to the window so you can take advantage of the increase in natural light.
12. *Paint it blue*: If you're serious about giving your office design a fresh, new look, a coat of fresh paint is the answer. Blue is the big colour this season, in

all kinds of soothing shades. Have a look at your local hardware or paint store and you're sure to find a shade that appeals to you. Whether or not you choose to repaint your small or home office, if you've worked through the other steps to organise your office, you've now got an office space that not only looks neater but will be easier to work in. And with the changes you've made, keeping your office organised will be easier, too.

2

HOW TO MANAGE MY OFFICE

2.1. DUTIES OF OFFICE MANAGER

An office manager's job description often includes pricing office supplies, managing payroll, controlling petty cash, supervising support staff and interviewing job applicants. An office manager must exercise sound judgment every day, and any lapse may mean termination. Equipment isn't the only thing that needs regular maintenance and support in an organisation. A large part of an office manager's job is motivating and coordinating others to ensure everyone is working together productively toward a common goal.

While an office manager often works under great pressure because her responsibilities are so great in scope, her satisfaction level is high, too. In a 2004 survey conducted by the International Association of Administrative Professionals (IAAP), office managers reported that being able to see the results of their labour reflected in increased productivity and office efficiency immediately is what they liked best about their job. An ideal office manager must have the following skills:

1. Top-notch computer skills.
2. Excellent phone demeanour.

3. *Verbal skills*: If an officer manager can't speak well, what kind of impression will she project? In many companies, foreign-language fluency is also an asset.
4. *Good written skills*: The ability to use proper grammar, syntax and logic when writing is crucial.
5. *Good organisational skills*: Not being able to find or access important information efficiently can hurt a business.
6. *Leadership qualities*: Office managers should be able to supervise others and have a willingness to use but not misuse power.
7. *A good work ethic*: Showing up on time and staying until the work is complete is also important.
8. *Team-playing skills*: The ability to share information where relevant and help make improvements.

If you're an administrative assistant interested in becoming an office manager, check with your human resources department for any related in-house training programmes available. Many large firms offer training and professional development courses to help prepare you for office management.

2.2. OFFICE MANAGEMENT PRINCIPLES

If chaos has crept into your small business—and is probably busy spreading throughout your organisation like a virus. Disorganisation and confusion are irritating, but they're also just plain bad for business. Think of it as a formula, if you like: chaos increasing equals profits decreasing. What to do? Control chaos by applying these basic office management principles:

2.2.1. Establish Office Management Routines and Stick to them

Routine tasks need routine procedures if you want to stay organised and keep things running smoothly. Set up routines for handling paperwork and office systems. For instance, every piece of paper that comes into your office should be handled once, acted upon, and filed – not haphazardly piled on a desk.

Office systems, such as computers, will need both administration and what I call panic mode procedures. When the system crashes or a computer-related piece of equipment fails, everyone in your office needs to know who to call and what not to do (such as try to fix the problem themselves). These data management articles provide helpful tips for everything from office filing systems through computer backup procedures.

2.2.2. Set up Clearly Delineated Responsibilities

Good office management depends on people knowing who is responsible for what—it's people who are accountable who get things done. What would happen, for example, if the purchasing for your small business was done by whoever whenever? Would you be able to find a paper clip when you wanted one?

Or print off a report when you needed to? Putting one person in charge of ordering all equipment and supplies solves the problem and keeps things running smoothly. It's the same with (computer) systems administration. You need to have one person responsible for the security of your computer system and keeping track of things such as accounts, passwords and software. Otherwise, chaos will proliferate.

2.2.3. Keep Records

Keeping records sounds like the easiest part of good office management – until you consider the need to keep those records both accessible and updated. But my first rule for controlling chaos will help you get a grip on this; make updating records an office routine. When you get a new customer or client, for instance, it only takes a moment to enter him into your contacts database. Then it will only take another moment or two to update the record after you've spoken to him on the phone.

2.2.4. Take a Walk through your Office and have a Sit

Is your office an example of space management or space mis-management? When you walk through the office, do you have to detour around obstacles or run the risk of tripping over something? When you sit down at a desk, could you actually work comfortably there? Are things logically arranged so that the things that you would use most at the desk are closest to hand? There are a lot of things crammed into offices nowadays, from printer stands through filing cabinets. For good office management, you need to be sure that all the things in the office are arranged for maximum efficiency and maximum safety.

2.2.5 Schedule the Scut Work

It's too easy to put off things that you don't like doing, and I don't know very many people that enjoy scut work. Unfortunately, an office, like a kitchen, won't function well without a certain amount of scut work being done. If you are a small business owner who's in the position of not being able to assign whatever you view as scut work to someone else, force yourself to get to it regularly by scheduling time each week for it. Take a morning or afternoon, for instance, and spend it making the cold calls or catching up on the accounting (or updating the records).

2.2.6. Delegate and Outsource

In a perfect world, everyone would only be doing what he or she had time to do and did well. As the world is not perfect, instead a lot of people are doing things that they don't have the time or talent to do well. Delegating and outsourcing cannot only improve your small business's office management, but free you to focus on your talents as well, thereby improving your bottom line. Virtual assistants can handle many of your office or administrative tasks.

2.2.7. Make Business Planning a Priority

Many small business owners spend their days acting and reacting and then wonder why they seem to be spinning their wheels. Business planning is an important component of good office management and needs to be part of your regular office management routine. Successful small business owners spend time every week on business planning, and many use daily business planning sessions as a tool for goal setting and growth. If you have staff, involve them in business planning, either formally or informally. Don't let chaos interfere with doing business. Once you start applying these seven principles of good office management, you'll be amazed at the difference good office management makes – and how much more business you do.

3

HOW TO SETUP MY OFFICE AT HOME

When you're thinking of starting a business at home, you first consider the nature of the business you want to open. Some types of businesses lend themselves to being run out of a home and others do not. An important issue to consider is whether your home business will disturb your neighbours or have an effect on the character of your neighbourhood. The following are more things to consider when thinking about what type of businesses lend themselves to being run out of the home:

1. Does the business require a lot of customer or client visits to your home; for example, tax return preparation or music lessons? Are there ways around this problem — for instance, could you visit the client's location instead?
2. Does the business require a lot of space for such purposes as inventory storage, order processing, or performing services — for example, auto repair?
3. Does the business produce undesirable side effects — for example, noise, air pollution, foul odours, excessive or toxic waste?

Some businesses are particularly well-suited for being run from the home:

1. Businesses customarily run in an office setting, such as desktop publishing, secretarial, bookkeeping and accounting, graphic design, and computer programming.
2. Service businesses, such as house cleaning, construction, or home repair work (concrete, carpentry, plumbing, etc.), particularly where you do the major part of the work at the customer's location.
3. Daycare businesses.

An important part of choosing whether to work at home is matching up what you want to do at home with what you can do at home. If you want to work at home, a good approach is to match up your skills and interests with a business need. Then ask yourself if that business need can be met through work done from a home workplace. After all, running your own business from home should be satisfying as well as profitable!

3.1. DEALING WITH CUSTOMERS

When you work at home you want to make sure that you and your business are taken seriously by customers, clients, and suppliers. You can do your part to ensure this happens by keeping the following points in mind:

1. Dress in a manner conducive to doing business in your chosen field whenever you think you might be meeting with customers, clients, and suppliers. If your business involves frequent or unexpected visits from members of these groups, you may have to dress this way all of the time.
2. When setting up your work area, make sure that customers, clients, and suppliers see a professional workspace, rather than someone's living area. You may want to have a separate entrance or even a separate structure for your business, if possible.

3. Answer your phone in a professional manner. If your home and business phone line are one and the same, you don't necessarily have to answer with your business name; a dignified "hello" is sufficient. The same principle applies to your answering machine message. If you can't answer your phone personally, you don't want potential customers, clients, or suppliers hanging up because they think they have the wrong number or because they're turned off by your message.

As a home business owner, you must be able to rely on your good reputation when you're dealing with customers and clients. Customers and clients who are happy with your service or products can get you more business through their good recommendations. If your customers and clients are not happy with you, while they may not bad-mouth your business, they're certainly not going to recommend it either! A few simple steps will go a long way in fostering good client and customer relations:

1. Deliver what you promise, whether it's a product or a service or a combination of the two.
2. Don't promise more than you can deliver. Let your customer or client be pleasantly surprised rather than disappointed.
3. Deliver your product or service in a timely manner. If you don't deliver on time, chances are you won't get paid on time!

If you need suppliers in order to run your business, you will want to create a relationship with them based on good faith and trust. Pay your bills on time! This simple act will foster a good relationship between you and your suppliers and they will be there when you need them to go the extra mile for you. If you need an order delivered right away or you need credit with another supplier, they'll be happy to vouch for you. If your suppliers provide you with reliable, timely service, you can provide your customers and clients with the same.

3.2. DEALING WITH FAMILY AND NEIGHBOURS

When you run a business out of your home, the issue of dealing with your neighbours, your friends, and your family comes to mind almost immediately. A traditional work setting contains natural boundaries for the people in your personal life. However, when you work at home you will need to create these boundaries so that your business, as well as your personal life, can run smoothly and successfully.

What can you do to create these boundaries? Mentally separating "home" from "office" is the first step you should take. A part of setting up these boundaries is deciding how to deal with interruptions from neighbours, friends, and family while you are working at home. Another issue you may confront when you work at home is neighbours, friends, and family asking for business-related favours. It's important to be ready with a plan to confront these "boundary" issues when they occur if you want you and your home business to be taken seriously and to succeed.

As a person who works at home, you will be faced with an issue that people who work in a traditional business setting are not. When you work at home, you have the task of conveying to those closest to you, your family, friends, and neighbours, that when you are at home and working, this is your place of business. People who would never dream of just barging into your workplace in a traditional business setting may see things differently when you work at home. They may see the fact that you're working at home as an opportunity to ask you to do errands, baby-sit, call you, or stop by just to chat.

In other words, if you're at home, you're not really working, at least in their mind. Because the clear distinction between home and workplace does not exist when you work at home, you must create the distinction. How can you get neighbours, family, and friends to take you seriously when you tell them you're working and can't be disturbed? Setting up a separate workspace helps, particularly if there's a door you can shut behind you. Even if this is possible, it probably isn't enough on its own.

When people try to interrupt you while you're working, whether it's in person or on the telephone, tactfully let them know that you can't be disturbed because you're working on something (tell them generally what it is), you're on a business call, you're with an employee, or you're in a meeting. Then let them know when you will be available and make sure it's outside your regular business hours. It may take some time, but your neighbours, friends, and family will learn to take your home business as seriously as you do!

When you work at home, you may find that neighbours, friends, and family feel free to ask you for discounts on your services and products or for free advice and merchandise. While someone close to you might not think of making this kind of request if you worked in a retail store or for a corporation, that same person feels that it's perfectly acceptable because your business is run from your home. What can you do? It doesn't hurt to remind those close to you that your livelihood (and in the case of your family, theirs as well!) depends on the success of your home business. The fact that your business is in your home doesn't make it any less of a business. Explain that if you give away your product or a service that you want others to pay for, you won't stay in business for very long.

While working at home can provide you with a freedom from structure not possible in a traditional work setting, it can also result in loneliness and lack of concentration. However, if you make a conscious effort, these common pitfalls of working at home can be overcome. Don't make the mistake of believing that working at home necessitates feeling lonely and out of touch with others in your line of work, particularly those who work in traditional settings. When you work from home, it's your responsibility to figure out what you need to run your business at its best and then take active steps to achieve those goals!

When you're working at home, it's easy to feel isolated. In a traditional work environment, you work and network with co-workers, you might commute back and forth to work with co-workers, and you might socialise with your co-workers at work or after hours. Working at home, especially if you don't have employees or co-workers, can be lonely. If you work at home, there are steps you can take to avoid feeling isolated and to make and maintain new business contacts:

1. Join professional groups such as industry organisations or associations.
2. Join professional groups for people working at home or people in small business.
3. Take classes in areas that are pertinent to your business and interest you.
4. Participate in and plan events that involve people in the business community.

Keep an eye open for business contacts and interaction wherever you are. Don't overlook the health club, the supermarket, the bookstore, or the neighbourhood block party as places where those with interests similar to yours will be found. Working at home can make it difficult to focus on your work. There are many distractions that don't exist in a traditional workplace such as chores and errands that need to be done and interruptions from friends, family, and neighbours. In the home workplace, guilty pleasures such as watching television or going to the beach on a beautiful, sunny day are very tempting. After all, there's no boss to answer to!

You can also stay focused on your work at home if you make every effort to set up a work area away from distractions. Stay away from the kitchen (unless your workplace is the kitchen!), away from rooms in your home where the television or radio are on in the background, away from areas where you are bothered by street and traffic noise, etc. Your tolerance for distractions is a highly individual matter. While some people can write an entire novel with a television blaring in the background, others need total silence to compose a sentence.

3.3. DRESSING CODE

When you are working at home, the dress code is up to you. But don't just assume that working at home means working in your bathrobe. Think about the way you do your best work. Can you focus on work, no matter what you're wearing? Or do shorts and a T-shirt make you feel like you should be at the beach? Are you more focused on your work when you're at your most comfortable with your lucky baseball cap on? Do you mentally feel "not at work" when you're not in attire that's totally presentable to the outside world?

When you are deciding how to dress in your home office, don't lose sight of the fact that a large part of your decision to work at home is largely based on the desire to make your own rules in your own workplace. Don't feel tied to the constraints of traditional work attire if you feel that you can be productive without it. The only person you have to impress is yourself! If you are meeting clients, customers, or suppliers, or have a meeting with your professional peers, dress according to the custom within your profession. When you're working at home there's no one to impress.

However, you don't want anyone else you deal with on a professional level to discount you or your business because it's a home business and they don't take you seriously because of the way you dress. This doesn't mean you should wear a suit when meeting with others if that's not the traditional dress for those in your field. In some fields, a person wearing khakis is dressed-up. In other lines of work, nothing but a business suit will suffice. Err on the professional rather than the casual side of dressing if you're not sure!

Working at home will make changes in most people's lifestyles. Here are some suggestions for getting physical exercise when you work at home:

— Join a health club with time and money saved from commuting.

— Organise or join a local sports team.

— Take up a sport you can do on your own, such as running, walking, or working with weights.

Your first inclination may be to say that a person who works from home doesn't have time for sports or an exercise programme. Nothing could be further from the truth! While it's understandable that you'll want to spend as much time as possible making your home business a success, you can't afford not to make time for physical fitness. Keeping fit helps keep you mentally alert, it gives you more stamina, and, if your sports activity involves others on a team or at a health club, it provides relief from the isolation you may experience working at home.

3.4. WORKING SCHEDULE

If contacting customers and suppliers is an important part of your business, you will want to set your work schedule according to their availability. When you start out in business, you may want to hold to the traditional business hours of your locale, or to the hours of your type of business. After you have been in operation for a while, you may get a feel for whether you could better serve customers and get an advantage over your competitors by adjusting your work schedule. You have much more freedom to choose your business hours if you don't speak directly with customers or suppliers.

If you work best in the wee hours of the morning, do it! Being your own boss was probably one of the reasons that you went into business for yourself. You should take advantage of this freedom when you can — you'll feel better about what you're doing and be more productive.

3.5. OFFICE SETTINGS

The area of your home where you operate your business — your workplace — will have an impact on the success of your business venture. To make sure that this impact is positive, you will need to organise it so that it becomes an efficient tool of your business. Your workplace should encourage productivity when you deal with customers or clients, suppliers, family, friends and neighbours, and yourself! Setting up such a work-conducive area requires wise choices of business and communication equipment and information sources, as well as accommodation to local zoning and other restrictions. And to avoid having your workplace unduly drain business profits that may not yet be there, this should all be done on a tight budget.

The two main ideas in creating a work space are functionality and cost. Your home office work area should allow you to perform all necessary duties of your business without unduly disrupting the functioning of the rest of your household, and should do so at a cost that does not put your new business too deeply in the hole. Most people working out of their homes find it helpful to have the work area somewhat isolated from the "personal" areas of the home. Whether you will find this true for you depends on what type of product or service your business provides, how you work best, and why you're working out of the home in the first place.

The type of product or service that your business provides often largely determines where your work space will be situated in your residence. If clients and customers will be coming into the work area, it's usually best to have it as isolated as possible from the rest of the house. Doing so helps establish that you "mean business." Also, to the extent possible, your work area should be situated where customers and clients will have to walk through as little of your personal space as possible. If feasible, a separate entrance to the work area might be best.

If your business involves working with power tools, other noisy equipment, or paint or other smelly solvents, it's probably the garage for you! But you still may want a desk or other work area where you can do your business's paperwork. Considering the type of business that you operate, all signals may point to selecting a work area in your house that is as isolated as possible from the functioning of the rest of the home. But before you set up your office in your attic or crawl space, remember why you chose to work out of your home. If you did so to care for your children or elderly parents, such isolation might not work out.

Possibly you have decided where to put your work area and are thinking that physical changes should be made to enhance its efficiency (partition walls, wood paneling, sound proofing, carpeting, etc.). All of these may be good ideas — and possibly some or all of these changes should be done — but the question is, when? If you are just starting your home business, economy and efficiency should be your watchwords. Expenses of doing business often are larger than anticipated, and income may not flow in as quickly as planned. Because of this, it's a good idea to hold your initial spending on physical facility items to those that are absolutely necessary to kick off and perform your business. You can always upgrade your work area when the profits roll in.

3.6. HOME OFFICE EQUIPMENT

For the most part, the suggestions for acquiring equipment, tools, furnishings, and other business assets are the same regardless of whether you work out of your home or in a separate business facility. Essentially, you should look at such acquisitions as investments of your valuable capital that will be made only after a careful analysis of your needs. You should avoid acquiring any item that won't make you and your business significantly more profitable, efficient, or productive. In planning your home office, keep in mind that some people have the preconceived notion that home businesses are not as committed or as efficient as other businesses.

So, if you bring customers or other people into your home work area, you should consider whether your desk, furnishings, and other equipment convey the right impression. Although these items usually don't have to be expensive or elegant, they may detract from your business image if they are battered or appear unbusinesslike. Your office equipment should convey the impression that you are serious (but not stodgy!) about your business, and you are able and willing to provide your customers with superior products or services.

3.7. HOME OFFICE SAFETY

If customers, suppliers, or employees visit your home business, you'll want to take all reasonable steps to make sure their visits are safe ones. Because your home business shares space in a home, your business visitors may not think to look for hazards that are a part of the home, but are not usually encountered in a business. Thus, if possible, you should try to keep your visitors out of the personal areas of the house where the belongings of family members may create hazards. Likewise, aggressive dogs or other animals should be kept away from visitors. Regardless of how hard you try to keep your business area safe for visitors, you should always have adequate liability coverage.

3.8. HOME BUSINESS REGULATION

In almost all countries of the world, there are laws to regulate home-based businesses. Violations of these laws can result in civil and criminal penalties as well as being forced to shut down the home workplace. Laws also may restrict the hiring of employees and outside contractors if they work out of their homes. While some localities have no zoning laws related to working at home, cities and towns that do have zoning laws usually prohibit or restrict working at home. The main rationale behind these prohibitive or restrictive zoning laws is to maintain the residential character of a neighbourhood. On the flip side, it is often illegal to live in some commercially zoned areas where you are running a business. Local zoning laws can impose many types of restrictions that will affect your ability to maintain a home office or business.

Some localities restrict the right of property owners to build separate structures. There may also be restrictions on how much of your home can be used exclusively for your home office or business. Local zoning laws can limit the number of employees you are allowed to have, or may not allow you to have any employees working in your home (other than domestics). Zoning ordinances may also affect your ability to advertise or run your business. Zoning rules may also impose environmental restrictions or prohibitions on home businesses. Noise, smoke, and odour can all be subject to zoning rules. Certain types of equipment are prohibited due to environmental concerns. The disposal of chemicals, hazardous substances, etc., may also be regulated by zoning. These restrictions may prevent you from operating certain types of businesses from your home.

4
HOW TO DETERMINE MY FACILITY NEEDS

If you are just getting into business, the decisions that surround the choice of a business facility can be particularly worrisome. Where do you start? Do you first decide the community in which you wish to locate the business, amassing all the information on it? Should you look at prospective sites and buildings, and imagine how well your business would operate in each? Should you look around for geographic areas not well served by potential competitors, then "hit 'em where they ain't?" These and many more inquiries deserve consideration as you search out a business facility.

To do this, you may wish to consider what small business owners generally look for in a business facility and how the facility can aid their businesses. As a small business owner, you can greatly increase the chances that you will acquire a business facility that will make a positive contribution to your bottom line if you carefully consider the functions that the facility must perform for your business.

4.1. EFFICIENT BUSINESS OPERATION

No matter what kind of business you have and how you

conduct it, if you own or rent a business facility apart from a home office, you do so in order to perform vital business functions there. This is true regardless of whether the facility houses your business headquarters and office, a retail store or a wholesale outlet, an inventory or equipment storage area, or a combination of several of these functions. Your search for the ideal facility will go much more smoothly — and will more likely be successful — if you are armed with a firm, fairly detailed idea about your facility requirements when you actually start the search.

If you are now in business. This may be a rather straightforward process if you are currently in business, and, for whatever reason, will be relocating. In this case, envisioning your replacement facility may be no more difficult than thinking about what aspects of your present facility you are satisfied with, and how you would improve upon those aspects that didn't measure up. It's likely this will be easier said than done, but at least you have had the valuable experience of seeing how your business ran out of the present facility.

Your proposed solutions to any facility problems may be theoretical, but they are grounded in what you have learned from running the business. If you are starting out. But what if you are just starting out in business? How do you go about making a wise choice for your business's first home? You may feel, however, that since you are just entering the business, you don't have a firm idea about what the operating steps of your business will be.

Although every small business is different, most small business owners will have to consider a number of issues in selecting a business facility. Not all of the listed items will be important to every small business, and the relative importance of each issue will also vary. Here is the list of common small business requirements that closely relate to the choice of an efficiently functioning business facility:

1. Provides space for all of your operating steps.
2. Is the right size, construction, condition, age, and interior layout.
3. Has dock and refuse facilities, if needed.
4. Is convenient for customers, suppliers, and employees.
5. Is situated in a supportive community.
6. Has beneficial business neighbours.
7. Has no environmental problems.
8. Has satisfactory security.
9. Can qualify for affordable insurance protection.

The bottom line is that your facility should do all that you want it to. If this is not the case, such as when business operations suffer because the facility is too cramped or inconveniently located, you may need to look for another facility, or investigate whether you can operate the business in such a way that minimises the deficiency of the facility.

4.2. MAPPING OUT THE OPERATING STEPS

Before you can determine what you will need from your business facility, you'll need to take a hard look at your business. What are the essential operating steps that you must do to bring your product or service to your customers? In what logical order should these steps be done? How many employees will you need? Will they be using specialised machinery? In thinking about this, don't forget about functions (such as marketing, billing, collection, payroll, and facility maintenance and security) that are necessary to support the essential steps. Once you have identified the essential business steps, you will want to think about how these steps (and related administrative functions) will translate into facility needs.

The process of mapping out your business's operating steps is designed to get you thinking about your facility needs. However, by itself, this process may not be enough. This is because when a business owner contemplates the operating steps of the business, he or she may concentrate too much on the physical structure of the business facility. However, in order to identify all of the business's needs relating to a facility, the business owner must also think about things beyond the structure, layout, and size of the facility. An example of such non-structural needs would be the selection of a location that is likely to bring in customers, without whom none of the essential business steps could be performed.

4.3. PHYSICAL STRUCTURE OF FACILITIES

The physical structure and layout of your facility should function as a tool that helps you to efficiently do all the things necessary to bring your business's products or services to its customers.

Retail and service businesses: Retail and services businesses that depend on customers coming into their facilities must place considerable emphasis on their appearance. The facility's exterior and interior design, decorating, and maintenance should make customers want to come into the business. Depending on the type of the business, the interior of the facility may be primarily set up to maximise efficiency (the idea being, "get them in, get them out"). This could be the objective of a tool rental business or a neighbourhood convenience food store. Or the facility could be set up to encourage customers to browse through the store, hopefully finding something to buy in addition to what they came into the store to get.

Retail and service businesses vary greatly in their facility size requirements and in their need for on-site inventory or supply storage. Businesses where customers are confined to a small sales area, and that have little or no inventory storage requirements, can exist in very small facilities. This is not the case for businesses where the customers must utilise a lot of space or where the items kept in inventory are large and numerous.

Wholesalers and manufacturers: Wholesalers and manufacturers generally do not have customers come into their facilities. Because of this, their facilities can be Spartan, although the effect of the facility's appearance on efficiency and employee morale should not be ignored. Wholesale businesses often require large, open facilities that put a premium on efficient material handling. This may take the form of wide aisles and storage racks that allow the use of lift trucks, large shipping and receiving docks, and a location that gives the facility good access to transportation facilities.

Small manufacturing businesses may not require any specialised facilities, their prime need usually being enough space for their supply storage, manufacturing processes, and product shipment. The facilities of manufacturers may need to be highly specialised to accommodate heavy machinery and assembly lines.

Modifications to building needed: Regardless of the type of your business, you may run into this situation. You find a facility that is well located, with a building that generally meets your requirements for size, layout, and appearance. In fact, the building is almost perfect. But, there is one thing about it that must be changed before you can use it. This could be something like adding or widening access doors, or increasing the capacity of the ventilation system.

4.4. DOCK AND REFUSE FACILITIES

Most small businesses don't have the volume of shipping

or receiving to require full-blown truck dock facilities. But if your business does ship or receive either a large number of truck-delivered items, or such items include those that are too large or heavy to be lifted off a truck bed and carried through a door, you probably need a dock facility. Some businesses, such as manufacturers, may in fact have separate shipping and receiving docks. If the flow of materials in and out of your facility is large, any inefficiency that comes about as a result of an inadequate dock facility may be passed along to other parts of your business.

Some small businesses have relatively small amounts of refuse, while others generate large amounts daily. If your business operation requires the disposal of food product or other organic waste, your disposal needs will be more acute. Large trash receptacles and trash compactors may be necessary. So don't agree to move into any facility until you know that you can obtain, and legally use, adequate refuse disposal equipment. If your business uses, generates, or receives toxic wastes or other environmentally damaging materials, there may be local, state, or federal disposal rules that your business must follow. Further, if you improperly dispose of hazardous materials on your facility site, federal law can require you to pay the costs of cleaning up the property.

4.5. CUSTOMERS AND SUPPLIERS

Every business depends on its customers for its very existence. To a greater or lesser extent, most businesses also rely on employees and a variety of suppliers who provide needed goods and services. Locating your business where these three groups can get to you easily is vital.

Customers: When you're ready to select the community in which to locate your business, you need to make sure that the chosen community provides ready access to enough potential customers to support your business. What constitutes "ready access" varies tremendously based on the type of business. A hot dog stand is extremely dependent on the number of people actually passing by; a manufacturer that sells only through wholesalers is not.

Suppliers: Unless your business provides purely services to customers, you depend on suppliers (distributors, wholesalers, manufacturers, etc.) to provide you with the items you need to create and market your product. Thus, all things being equal, it's usually better from the point of view of delivery and price to be close to your important suppliers.

Employees: For many small businesses, the ability to attract and retain qualified employees can be critical to success. Because of this, you should carefully consider the availability of qualified employment prospects within a half-hour drive of your location.

4.6. NEARBY BUSINESSES

Business that sell their products or services to customers at the business facility have a strong interest not only in the general character of the neighbourhood, but in the kind and appearance of nearby businesses and neighbours. This consideration is less important to businesses that don't have as many on-the-premises contacts. However, just as a business should never completely disregard the appearance of its facility, it should not completely overlook the effect that the appearance of surrounding businesses and neighbours may have on how it is perceived.

Strictly from an appearance standpoint, what would you like your customers to see as they approach your facility? Usually, you'll want your facility and surrounding buildings to roughly fit in with each other visually. Within some settings, however, a bit of tasteful architectural difference from other buildings may make your building more visible. Proximity to magnet stores. By deciding where to locate your business, you in effect get to pick the appearance of nearby businesses and other neighbourhood buildings, and may be able to "piggy-back" on a neighbour's ability to draw customers to the area.

Many small businesses may benefit by being close to a "magnet" store, that is, a large store that attracts a large number of customers. If you operate a retail or service business that depends on customers coming to your premises, you may want to position your facility on an access route to the magnet store. By doing so, you can greatly increase the number of potential customers who walk or drive by your facility. Although any business that attracts large numbers of customers to an area can serve as a magnet for nearby stores, whether the magnet will benefit your store will depend on whether it competes with your business, and whether its operation and target clientele are compatible with yours.

If you have determined that you will benefit from a nearby magnet store, there are other things that you can do — other than just being there — that can enhance these benefits. You may wish to consider adjusting your store hours to coincide with that of the magnet. If possible, think about opening your store a little earlier and closing it a little later than the magnet. This way, your store could benefit from customers arriving before the magnet's opening, as well those who would walk or drive by your store shortly after the magnet's closing. Depending on your business, the magnet store's employees might be among your early and late customers.

For some kinds of businesses, such as wholesalers or mail order retailers, the physical closeness of competitors really doesn't matter much. Their customers usually don't go to the facility to place an order, so they'll never see a competitor located directly across the street. If this describes your business situation, you may be able to ignore the question of nearby competitors. In certain instances, competitors may "cluster" in close proximity for the betterment of all. This may be done where several stores selling unique, but similar, items cluster so as to draw more customers than any one store could hope to.

Art, jewellery, and high-fashion clothing stores are examples of retailers that may find it advantageous to locate close to business competitors for this reason. Competitors may also cluster to cut expenses. For example, two heavy construction companies are located next to each other on a private gravel road that is some distance to the nearest paved country road. Each uses the gravel road to haul their heavy machinery to the country road. By sharing the considerable costs necessary to maintain the gravel road, each of the two companies is able to reduce its cost of doing business, without giving a competitive advantage to its "neighbour."

4.7. SECURITY ISSUES

Crimes against people and crimes against property can significantly add to your cost of doing business for many types of small businesses. Shoplifting, employee theft of inventory (sometimes euphemistically called "asset shrinkage"), and theft of business property are all too common and costly. Crimes against business owners, employees, customers, and others who enter the premises are less common, but can be more tragic and traumatic when they occur. While you'll never be completely free from the effects of crimes against your business, there are decisions that you can make about your facility that can lessen the likelihood and impact of crime on your business. Primarily, these decisions concern facility location and building security.

Depending on the severity of threats your business faces, you may find it advisable to augment your building security features by using security guards. You can either employ such guards directly, or contract with private security service companies for them. Although you can have a guard stationed at the site around the clock, most small businesses that use security services opt for a guard that periodically checks the facility after hours. Leaving trained guard dogs to roam the locked facility after closing is another alternative.

4.8. INSURANCE PROTECTION

No matter what kind of business facility you have, or where it is located, you will need insurance coverage to protect your business from property damage and liability risks. You will need insurance to protect your business against personal injury and other liability claims arising from your use of the facility. You'll also need coverage to reimburse the business for any property damage to the building and its contents caused by fire, wind, lightning damage, and the like, as well as damage caused by the acts of people, such as theft, vandalism, and negligent damage to your business property.

4.9. IMPORTANCE OF BUSINESS FACILITIES

All things being equal, a business facility that can accommodate potential future growth would be more attractive than one that does not. However, realistically, all things are rarely equal. If one facility offers more room, you can expect to pay for it some way: in price, location, or other terms or features. If this is true, does it make sense to pay now for the benefit of easy expansion later? It may, but only if you reasonably believe (not just hope) that you will need the extra space in the not-too-distant future and that any additional costs that go along with this extra space will not be an undue drag on current business growth.

Most small business advisers suggest that startup businesses keep a tight rein on costs. Business plans can be put together that envision additional facility requirements, but actually acquiring the additional space should probably be put on hold until business activity and profits justify taking on the added expense.

If your facility allows you to efficiently carry out the necessary functions of your business, presents the business in a good light, and allows for growth potential, you're well on your way to having made a good facility choice. However, there is one more important attribute of the "ideal" facility: it should fulfil your space needs economically.

If you are not able to purchase or rent your facility at the best price, your business will be at a lasting disadvantage. The misspent facility money will be a drag on your company's profitability, which can have several effects. In the all-important startup phase, this money won't be there for other needed expenses. Also, overspending on the facility will make your company's profit and loss statement less attractive, which can make it more difficult for the business to borrow money.

How do you determine if the price is right for a particular property? An independent real estate appraiser with a good knowledge of business property in the area could be a help. But don't forget that there are really two separate "price" issues here. The first is what is the property worth on the open market. The second — and most important for you — is what can you afford to pay for the property, considering your evaluation of your business's profit potential. The commercial real estate broker can help you with the first question; you'll have to wrestle with the second one. Here are some ideas for saving facility dollars, particularly if you're in the startup or early childhood of your business:

1. *Start out in a home office*: Some types of businesses can be started out of and run from the home at least on a small scale. If your proposed business is one of them, you may want to try this. Operating a home office can help you to learn the business and build up a core of customers before you commit yourself to the overhead costs of a separate facility.
2. *Share space with others*: Certain startup businesses are able to keep down their overhead expenses by sharing space, telephone, and secretarial services with like businesses. While these arrangements need not end as the startup phase ends, with time, one or more of the businesses may require a disproportionate share of the space and services, or may outgrow the office altogether.
3. *Locate within a business incubator*: Business incubators are groups that are designed to help small businesses survive and succeed through the startup phase of their existence. Business incubators go several steps beyond the idea of shared space and office services; they also provide management and financial assistance. Although incubators have shown themselves to greatly improve a startup business's chances of success, not all types of businesses benefit equally from incubators. Because incubators are usually located in low-rent, often out-of-the-way facilities, they tend to work best when your business does not need to be at a particular location in order to draw in-store customers.

5

HOW TO SELECT THE RIGHT FACILITY

If you have put in the time and effort — and possibly the pain — of identifying your business's operating steps, and have used this information to determine your facility needs, you may be more than ready to hit the road to find your facility. But, before you do this, a few words about the method of your search. Start by choosing the general area in which you want to locate. Many a small business owner picks out a business facility this way:

Real estate agents: If you know the areas where you are looking like the back of your hand, know how to ferret out commercial properties for sale, can invest a good bit of time in the search, and are knowledgeable about local commercial real estate practices, you may be able to locate an acceptable property by yourself, or with the help of real estate agents representing sellers. If all of this doesn't describe you, you may want to employ your own real estate agent.

Time can save money: If you can avoid it, don't start your facility search so late that you feel rushed to make a decision. Unless you take the time to see and evaluate several properties, you run a higher risk of making a costly mistake. Once you have tentatively decided on a property, revisit it a few more times; at different times of the day, if possible. You'll never know what you may find out.

5.1. HOW TO DECIDE WHICH FACILITY IS BEST

Assuming you have done all your homework and have effectively conducted a search that has narrowed down your choice to a few properties, how do you decide which facility is best? There are two general methods of evaluation that can be used.

A non-numeric method: This process is simple to describe, but not so simple to do. For each separate property, consider how that property would (or would not) meet each of your facility needs, and consider the relative importance of each such need. Then compare your results for each facility, and decide, on the whole, which property most completely meets your business needs. The biggest danger in using this method is that it lets you over-focus on some items, while under-focusing, or ignoring others.

If you're generally the optimistic type, you may have the tendency to over-value the property with the biggest positive aspects, even if it also has more important negative aspects. The contrary may be true if you are generally a pessimist: the existence of a few relatively negative features in a property may obscure its other, more important positive features.

A numeric scoring system: The following numeric scoring system uses everything that was considered in the non-numeric system, but adds scoring elements in the hope of making its results clearer and more objective. The idea is to first assign a value (say from 1 for very poor, to 10 for very good) based on your evaluation of how well the property fulfils each of your facility needs. Then you assign a value (say from 1, low, to 10, high) to how important this facility need is to the operation of your business. Finally, you multiply these two numbers for each facility need, and add up the results. The resulting answer for each separate facility can give you some idea of how well-suited the various properties are for your need.

To illustrate this method, this is a simplified example property "X":

Facility Needed	Importance of Need	How Well It Meets Need	Score
Location	3	9	27
No competition	5	7	35
Condition of building	3	6	18
Price	5	7	35
Security features	9	4	36
Total			151

One possible weakness to the numeric comparison is that it could lead one to over-inflate the relative worth of the property earning the highest score. If for instance, if property "A" receives a total of 460 points, and property "B" receives 450 points, does it really mean that "A" is better than "B"? Probably the two are close enough that this 10 point spread doesn't really have much significance.

Assuming that you have determined your facility needs and have chosen the right facility, you're now ready to make the decision about whether to buy or rent the property. The rent-or-buy decision can also arise if you are selecting from a group of competing sites, some of which are for sale and others which are for lease.

To help you make this decision, you need to consider:

1. When leasing makes sense.
2. When buying makes sense.

3. Common lease terms.
4. Comparing the economics.

If you are a new business owner considering whether to acquire a facility by purchase or by lease, you may have a tendency to concentrate on the short-term, such as the first year cash flow projections that would result for each of the alternatives. This is natural, and probably altogether necessary: If things don't go well enough in the first couple of years of the business's operation, it may not be around to see how a particular decision would have benefited it 10 years down the road. But having said this, it's still worthwhile to consider how a lease or rental could affect your business in the future.

The following factors, if relevant to your situation, may lead you to conclude that you should lease, rather than purchase, your business facility.

1. *Your current cash flow is of vital importance* — Particularly in the early years, a lease may be better than a purchase from a cash flow perspective. This is because up-front outlays associated with a lease are usually less than those required with a property purchase. With a lease, your main initial cash expense may well be limited to your security deposit, plus first rent payment. With a purchase, you have to have the lump-sum purchase price, or at least a down payment on a mortgage.
2. *You don't want maintenance duties* — Many leases place the duty of maintaining the property on the landlord. Examples of such maintenance can include the things that are necessary to ensure the continued structural soundness of the building (such as roof repairs and periodic maintenance, tuck-pointing, maintenance of heating and cooling, electric, and plumbing equipment), and those that go to the facility's ease of use and appearance.

3. *You want to retain your mobility* — Maybe you're not sure that the facility that you will select now will serve your needs several years in the future. You may need more or less space, your target market may have moved elsewhere, or better-suited properties may later be built.
4. *Your company's credit rating may not support a mortgage* — If your business is rather new, or has experienced some financial difficulties, lenders may not be willing to extend it sufficient credit for a mortgage on the facility. With the same financial situation, however, a property owner may well be willing to rent a property to your business.
5. *You haven't found a suitable property to buy* — You may want to buy, but have found that all properties that would be suitable for your needs have been offered only on a lease basis.
6. *The facility may be in an area of declining real estate values* — You may find a facility that meets your needs, but you are concerned that the real estate values in the area are stagnate, or may actually drop in value. In this case, leasing makes sense: let the landlord suffer the effect of the declining values, not you!
7. *A lease may bring you tax savings* — The money you pay in rent is deductible as a business expense. Depending on several factors, such as how long you have been in business, how profitable your business has been, and what portion of the purchase price or rent relates to land itself — rather than to buildings — a lease is likely to cut your near-term tax bill when compared with a purchase.

The following factors, if relevant to your situation, may lead you to conclude that you should purchase, rather than lease, your business facility.

1. *You want control of the property* — Maybe you intend to make substantial additions or renovations to the property. Or you decide to change your business hours or change something else about the way you are doing business. If you rent your facility, you may have to get your landlord's permission to make these changes. If, however, you own the property, there will be no one looking over your shoulder to question your moves.
2. *You can consider the long-term cost* — A lease may sometimes beat out a purchase in terms of cash flow, particularly in the early years. But over the long haul, a purchase is usually cheaper because a landlord, in addition to paying all of the costs associated with purchasing and maintaining the property, will attempt to build in a profit for himself. You can avoid paying this profit premium by buying, rather than renting, the property.
3. *You want to stay at the same location* — For some businesses, such as certain retail and service businesses, location is all important. If you have established a winning business location, you don't want to lose it because of a rent escalation or because the landlord just wants the property for another use. If you own the facility, you won't have these worries.
4. *You haven't found a suitable property to lease* — You may want to lease, but have found all properties that would be suitable for your needs have been offered only for sale, rather than lease.
5. *You are in an area of appreciating land values* — If you will locate in an area where you think land values will continue to increase, it would be better to own the property rather than to rent it. This is would be particularly true if you are able to spot this real

estate trend before prices jump up in recognition of it.

6. *A purchase may bring you tax savings* — Although, unlike rent, the money you use to purchase your facility is not deductible, you are allowed to recover this outlay over time by yearly depreciation deductions. If you financed your purchase, interest-paid deductions are also available. Depending on several factors, such as how long your have been in business, how profitable your business has been, and what portion of the purchase price or rent relates to the land itself — rather than to buildings — a purchase may actually cut your tax bill when compared with a lease.

5.2. LEASE PROVISIONS

If you have decided that you would rather lease your business facility than purchase it, you should familiarise yourself with the following terms and provisions that are commonly found in commercial leases.

1. *Gross lease*: This is the most traditional type of lease: the tenant pays rent; the landlord pays taxes, insurance, and maintenance expenses relating to the property. Increasingly, gross leases contain escalation clauses, which provide that the amount of rent is to be adjusted to offset increased expenses.
2. *Net lease*: A net lease transfers some or all of the expenses that the landlord is traditionally responsible for to the tenant. With a single net lease, the tenant pays rent plus taxes relating to the tenant's portion of the property. Under a double net lease, the tenant also pays its proportional part of insurance premiums. Finally, with a triple net lease, the tenant pays all charges payable under a double net lease, plus maintenance expenses.

3. *Fixed lease*: A fixed lease provides for a fixed amount of rent over a fixed rental period (term). These types of leases usually seem the least threatening for the small business owner tenant, since you don't obligate yourself today for rent increases in the future. But, there is a downside to a fixed lease: if you want to renew the lease when it expires, the landlord may choose to raise rent sharply, particularly if your business appears to be doing well, and would suffer from relocating elsewhere. If your initial lease term was short, you might end up wishing that you had opted for a longer term lease with fixed or determinable rent increases.
4. *Step lease*: A step lease provides for set rent increases to take effect at stated times. This will provide you with the peace of mind of knowing what your rental amounts will be for a longer time period, while giving the landlord some protection against rising costs. If you are considering renting a facility under a step lease, carefully consider whether each of the scheduled rent increases is reasonable. Are the increases out of line with historic consumer price indexes or local rental increases?
5. *Percentage lease*: With a percentage lease, your landlord shares in your good (or bad) fortune. The lease provides for a fixed amount of rent, plus an additional amount that is set as a percentage of your gross receipts or sales.
6. *Lease term*: Identifies how long the lease will be in effect. If you suspect that you will want to stay at this same business location beyond the initial term, try negotiating the inclusion in the agreement of a renewal option that entitles you to renew the lease for a specified period and a specified rent.

7. *Rental rate*: Tells how much the rent is and when it must be paid. Most leases also include late payment provisions that impose additional charges if you fail to pay the rent when it's due or within a specified grace period. If your business experiences seasonal or irregular sales activity, try negotiating a flexible rental rate that corresponds to the changes in your cash flow.
8. *Escalation clause*: This clause provides for increases in rent over a specified time period. The escalations can be fixed, or determined with reference to an outside factor, such as increases in the landlord's operating costs, increases in a cost index, or increases in the tenant's gross receipts or sales.
9. *Maintenance*: Specifies who is required to maintain which portions of the building and land. If you are responsible for doing so, the lease should say whether you can contract with anyone of your choosing to provide these services, or whether the service providers have to be approved by the landlord.
10. *Competition*: In the case of a lease of retail space, such as a store in a shopping mall, there may be restrictions placed on the landlord's right to lease nearby space to businesses similar to your business.
11. *Subletting*: Spells out whether, and under what conditions, you are entitled to sublease the premises to another. Remember, if you sublet the property, you normally will still be liable for paying the rent if the subletting tenant does not pay.
12. *Improvements and modifications*: Identifies whether you have the right to make improvements or modifications to the facility so that it better suits your needs.

13. *Taxes*: Specifies who is responsible for the real property taxes.
14. *Insurance and liability*: Fixes who is responsible for casualty and liability insurance and how much coverage must be carried. Also may contain language that says under what circumstances, if any, the parties to the contract will excuse each other for liability for injury to persons, or to the property.
15. *Renewal option*: Specifies whether the tenant has the option to renew the lease when it expires and, if so, specifies the amount of rent to be paid for the renewal lease term. A renewal option can give your business protection against your landlord's wanting to hit you with an unreasonably large rent increase when your first lease term expires.
16. *Purchase option*: Tells whether you'll have the right or obligation to purchase the facility at the end of the lease term. This provision should specify an option price or range and how and when the option may be exercised.
17. *Destruction or condemnation*: States whether the landlord is required to rebuild if the property is destroyed. Specifies whether rent will be abated, and whether you can terminate your lease obligations if the facility is totally or partially destroyed. This provision will specify what rights you and your landlord enjoy if the facility is taken by eminent domain.
18. *Landlord's solvency*: A useful provision from your point of view, which spells out your rights as a tenant if your landlord's mortgage company forecloses on the leased premises
19. *Zoning and land use restrictions*: Specifies what zoning or other restrictions apply to the building.

20 *Tenant "going dark" rights*: A fear of many small tenants in a shopping centre is that a major tenant will go out of business or not renew its lease("going dark"). In the present economic climate, in which major department stores are filing for bankruptcy and closing stores, this is a real problem.

5.3. ADVANTAGES OF LEASING

The main advantage of leasing a business facility is that your initial outlay of cash to gain the use of an asset is generally less for leasing than it is for purchasing. However, perhaps the main advantage of purchasing is that you end up paying out less in the long term than you would have paid if you leased the facility. Moreover, if you purchase, you get the benefit of any appreciation in the value of the property. A cash flow analysis provides an estimate of how much cash you would need to set aside today to cover the after-tax costs of each facility acquisition alternative. To perform the analysis, you need to know or assume certain facts, including:

1. Purchase and financing terms, including closing costs.
2. Lease terms.
3. Your combined central and state income tax rate.
4. The facility's expected useful life to your business, for depreciation purposes.
5. The asset's estimated value, when you sell it, or at the end of its useful life to your business.
6. Your cost of capital.
7. Any other costs that you would incur if you leased the facility but not if you purchased it, or vice versa.

6

EQUIPPING MY OFFICE

The type of business you operate will in large part dictate what equipment and other fixed assets you'll require to properly run your business. We can't say what exactly you should acquire without first knowing what you'll be doing. However, we can provide some general points that you may want to consider before you acquire any business asset. You shouldn't acquire any equipment or other fixed assets that your business really doesn't need. By their nature, fixed assets represent relatively long-term investments of capital. In most cases, your recovery of the money you spend in acquiring the assets will span several years.

Accordingly, unless you have unlimited financial resources, you should avoid acquiring any asset that you can't reasonably say will bring a significant increase in your profits, efficiency, or productivity over the course of the asset's useful life in your business. Be especially careful about tying up capital in fixed assets in response to short-term needs. You'll also usually be well-served to focus on functionality over form in addressing your needs. For example, a prior job may have left you with the feeling that an ornate desk and a set of limited edition lithographs are necessary to give your office an air of professionalism.

Upon closer examination, however, you may easily conclude that you'll be just as effective, and have more money available in your operating budget, with less expensive furnishings and artwork. For an item that is relatively inexpensive, you may be able to resolve the acquisition decision by honestly assessing whether the item is something your business really needs as opposed to an item that you merely want or think you need. For a major asset acquisition, however, you should commit yourself to performing a thorough cost-benefit analysis to determine whether the expected acquisition and operational costs will be fully recovered through expected increases in earnings or savings over the asset's life. It goes without saying that this analysis must be done before you proceed with the acquisition because you'll rarely make a profit when disposing of a non-productive asset.

6.1. COMMUNICATIONS EQUIPMENT

Unless you're planning to rely solely on face-to-face meetings to keep in touch with customers, suppliers, and others with whom you deal, your business is going to need some communications equipment. Among the items that you may have to obtain or select for your business are:

- — A telephone system.
- — A long-distance phone company.
- — Answering machines or services.
- — Business listing for your phone number.
- — A facsimile machine.
- — Mail and package delivery.

6.1.1. Telephone System

The telephone is absolutely vital to the running of most

every business. Your business is truly unique if you really believe that it could survive without this tool for staying in contact with your customers, suppliers, and the rest of the world. Among your first tasks in setting up your business's telephone system will be to select long-distance service providers and the telephone features you want. Within the last several years, features that traditionally have been available only for sophisticated telephone systems of large companies have become available to small businesses.

As with any other business expense, you shouldn't spend money for any of these features if your business doesn't truly need them. A penny saved is as good as a penny earned! If you infrequently speak to customers or suppliers, you may not need any of these features. In contrast, if the conduct of your business requires that you be able to instantly talk to all customers or suppliers who call, without the fear of missing a call, you should consider purchasing call waiting or a multiline system, an answering machine, and possibly a cellular phone.

Your local phone company may provide you with an attractive alternative to purchasing your own phone system by offering special services for businesses. In general, these services allow you to lease equipment with the features you want, with the phone company assuming the responsibility for maintaining your overall system. Even if you don't need a sophisticated telephone system, your local phone company can provide a variety of services on "regular" phone lines. These include capabilities like conferencing and voice mail, which competes with an answering machine, but takes messages while your phone is in use.

6.1.2. Long-Distance Company

How should you go about finding the right long-distance

service provider for your company? If you're already in business, reviewing your old phone bills should give you a pretty good idea of your calling patterns. If you don't have the benefit of old phone bills, do your best to answer the following types of questions:

— How often will I be making long-distance calls?

— How long will my calls generally last?

— When will I primarily be making the calls?

— Where will I primarily be calling?

Upon completing this analysis, contact some long-distance companies and describe your calling patterns. Then compare the plans that each company offers to address your specific needs. Obviously, cost will be a prime factor, so you'll want to be on the lookout for hidden fees and charges. Is a high monthly fee the trade-off for a low calling rate? Will an amazing discount rate apply only after you've made a minimum dollar amount of calls? Will your business discount apply to calls that aren't made from your office?

Although cost is important, don't discount the quality and reliability of a provider's services. A great rate won't be much good if your calls don't go through, if the lines are garbled, or if you can't get immediate attention from a service technician should you need assistance. On the other hand, in most areas every long-distance provider offers the same excellent service, and there really isn't any noticeable difference among them.

6.1.3. Answering Machines and Services

Unless you can afford to miss telephone calls and the potential business they may represent, you must have some kind of telephone answering service in place at your business. Call waiting, while useful, is not a complete substitute for an answering service because there will be times when you're not around to pick up the phone or when you'll decide it's inappropriate to interrupt a conversation to take another incoming call.

A simple answering machine or a voice mail service provided by your local telephone company will usually do the trick. Because answering machines won't pick up calls when you're on the phone, voice mail may be the way to go if you have only one phone line. In any event, when shopping for a business answering machine or voice mail service, one feature you should probably demand is variable length message recording. This enables your callers, and not the machine, to determine when their messages to you are finished. Another useful feature is remote access, which enables you to listen to your messages from any phone.

Once you have an answering service in place, record an outgoing message that identifies your business and its normal hours of operation and that clearly instructs callers on when they should start their message. Keep your message short and to the point to avoid further frustrating a caller who in all likelihood expected to be talking to a live human voice.

6.1.4. Business Listing of Home Phones

Depending on the telephone company that provides your service and the particular law in the state where you reside, you may be required to list your home telephone as a business telephone if you do any work out of your home. If this happens, you should expect to see your telephone bill rise because the rates for business phone services are generally higher than those for residential services. Just what level of business activity will make it necessary for you to list as a business varies from telephone company to telephone company and from state to state.

It's pretty safe to say that you will be required to list your telephone as a business if you include your home telephone number in advertisements. Beyond this, you may have to have a business listing if you include a home telephone number as a business number on any company materials distributed to the public (such as stationery or business cards). Some states will even require you to get a business listing if you do business over a home telephone! If you are in doubt about whether you'll need a business telephone listing or not, you can always ask your telephone company. But you may end up regretting doing this if the answer is not what you wanted or if you disagree with how the telephone company is applying its rules or interpreting the law.

Instead of asking the telephone company, you may be able to get the needed information by consulting a network of local business owners. While the likely higher rates of a business listing are the downside, such a listing can also help grow your business. It gives your business higher visibility in the "white pages" and allows you to gain access to the yellow pages, which can be an excellent marketing tool for your business.

6.1.5. Facsimile Machines

The ability of facsimile (fax) machines to instantly send and receive documents have made them fixtures in the modern office. Contracts, orders, letters, and other time-sensitive documents that businesses previously sent by courier or next-day delivery services can now be transmitted over the telephone lines at a fraction of the cost and in a fraction of the time. Of course, whether you in fact need a fax machine is really dependent on the nature of your business. If you don't envision sending or receiving a lot of faxes, you may be better off finding a local package depot, copy shop, or other business that provides facsimile services. Or, if you expect that you'll primarily be faxing documents created on your computer, a fax/modem may adequately meet your needs. In assessing your need for a fax machine, keep in mind that communicating by fax is now a favoured method of doing business in most quarters. Accordingly, you should consider whether the lack of a fax machine will adversely affect your dealings with customers, suppliers, and others who may be accustomed to doing business by fax. If you're going to have a fax machine and you depend on not missing any phone calls, you probably should have a two-line telephone system. This is because if you have only one line, no one will be able to get through to speak to you while the fax machine is sending or receiving.

6.1.6. Mail and Package Delivery

For most businesses, mail and package delivery services are important business tools. If you plan to make use of such services, you'll want to consider both how you should receive deliveries (P.O. box or street address) and how you should send them. Choosing a P.O. box or street address. This first issue is of particular concern if you run your business out of your home.

Another reason to consider using a street address, even if you also list a P.O. box, relates to public perceptions. Because some unscrupulous people have run fraudulent mail order operations from P.O. box addresses, some people view a business that only lists a P.O box address with suspicion. If you give them a street address, they may have some measure of comfort that you actually can be found if they have a future problem with a product or service that you provided.

6.2. IMPORTANCE TO KEEP A COMPUTER IN YOUR OFFICE

A computer can help you to become more organised, to work more efficiently, and to accomplish many tasks that otherwise would likely require professional assistance. However, don't rush out to purchase a computer without first determining how you specifically intend to use it to aid your business. Otherwise, you may find that you've tied up excess capital in a system that does far more than you really need or, even worse, that you've acquired a system that doesn't accomplish what you expected and that ends up being a rather expensive paperweight.

A good first step in assessing your computer needs is to list which tasks you believe would be more efficiently performed if computerised. Labour-intensive tasks such as recordkeeping, computing payroll, invoicing, analysing financial projections, writing letters, and preparing advertisements and promotional materials are prime candidates. It's a good idea to speak with other business owners to find out how they are using computers to assist their business and to leverage their time.

You should also ask yourself if you're really ready to invest not only your money, but also your time in learning to use the computer in your business. Rest assured that if you do decide to take the plunge, you're going to be spending many an hour just becoming familiar with even the most user friendly of computers and programmes and incorporating the computer into your daily routine. Performing this assessment may convince you that you really don't need a computer at all or at least at the present time. Then again, you may conclude that you shouldn't be working without one.

For a computer to accomplish the tasks you desire, you must supply it with the proper applications software. Applications software are computer programmes that instruct the computer on how to perform specific functions. You can purchase the most expensive business computer available, but it won't do much for your business if the software it's running doesn't do what you want. You can run into a similar problem if the computer you acquire isn't capable of effectively running your desired software.

Accordingly, it's frequently better to determine which software applications you'll be using before you decide what computer hardware to acquire. The most basic kind of software is operating system software, which is a programme such as one of Microsoft's Windows iterations - 98, ME, NT, 2000, XP etc. - that controls the computer's monitor, disk drives, printer, and other components and also controls how the components work with your applications software. Most computers come with the most up-to-date version of this software preloaded.

The physical equipment that comprises a computer system represents the system's "hardware." The basic hardware components of any computer are the central processing unit, a monitor, a keyboard, disk and hard drives, and a printer. Other common business components include CD-ROM and DVD drives, modems, and scanners. Which of these components you'll actually need will depend largely on the types of software programmes you choose to run and the types of tasks you want to accomplish.

1. *Central Processing Unit (CPU)*: The CPU controls the speed at which the computer processes information. The primary factor in this speed is the CPU's processing chip. For example, a computer running a Pentium 4 chip will generally be faster than a computer running a Pentium III chip. For a given type of chip, a higher gigahertz (GHz) value will equate to greater speed. For example, a 2.0 GHz Pentium system will generally be faster than a 1.2 GHz Pentium system. Another important factor in a computer's speed is the amount of its random access memory (RAM). RAM, which is measured in megabytes (MB), is where your computer

temporarily stores information being used by programmes it's currently running. To effectively run new software applications, you really need a computer with at least 128 MB of RAM, although having 512 MB RAM or even 1024 MB is quickly becoming preferable.

2. *Monitor*: This is the television-type screen at which you'll be staring for countless hours as you do your work. As you compare monitors, you'll run across references to screen size, refresh rates, dot pitch, and other strange terms. The key is to find a monitor that you can read without undue eyestrain. The size of the monitor is also important. The larger the monitor, the easier it is to read. And the flat screen monitors are slick, albeit still somewhat pricey.
3. *Keyboard*: As is the case with the monitor, the key issue in comparing keyboards is your comfort in using them. Ergonomic keyboards that place the keys in what is believed to be a more natural alignment for your fingers to access are available. A supplement to the keyboard for entering work and executing commands is the mouse. These also come in various styles, so you should look for one that's comfortable and easy to use. You can choose a wireless keyboard and mouse and avoid all those cords and cables.
4. *Disk drives*: A computer uses disk drives to read information from and store information to floppy diskettes. Drives used to come in 51/4" and 31/2" sizes, although the former have been consigned to the technological graveyard and the latter are headed in that direction.
5. *Hard drives*: The hard drive is where your computer stores programmes and other information on a

somewhat permanent basis. The amount of available space is measured in gigabytes. With software applications continuing to grow in size, you're usually best off getting as large a hard drive as you can afford. In fact, you probably should avoid starting out with a hard drive of less than 40 GB.

6. *Printers*: Your options for a printer range from rather slow and inexpensive (inkjet printers) to fast and more expensive (laser printers). In comparing the costs of different printers, it's important to look beyond just the initial purchase price. For example, if a particular printer requires special paper, find out how much that paper costs. Also consider how much it will cost to replace the printer's ink supply and how frequently you'll be incurring that cost. Apart from cost and features, an important factor in deciding what type of printer your business needs is who will be seeing the documents you print out.
7. *CD-ROM drives*: A CD-ROM drive runs applications and retrieves information stored on compact discs, which are capable of holding large quantities of data. Some CD-ROM drives are also able to store information to CDs. Ideally it's nice to have a CD-ROM with RW (read and write) capabilities. If you will be keeping financial or other records that must be retained in electronic format, some sort of backup should be used to safeguard your information. You can use your CD-ROM drive as a tool for backing up the computer's hard drive.
8. *Modems*: A modem is the device that enables your computer to communicate with other computers over the telephone lines and to ride the information superhighway. With most modems currently on the

market, you can also use your computer to send and receive computer documents by fax. In shopping for a modem, the main feature to look for is its transmission rate (56K bps is good), because that determines how quickly a file can be transmitted and how long your phone line will be tied up. Higher transmission speed alternatives other than regular phone lines are offered by telephone (DSL) companies and cable modem companies. These "broadband" alternatives are certainly preferable if you can afford them.

9. *Scanners*: A scanner is used to quickly input an existing written document or photograph into your computer. The scanner converts the item into a computer file that you can then edit or manipulate. If you think you need a scanner, be sure to "try before you buy." Check out the quality of the scanned image and confirm that the corresponding file is in a format that's compatible with your existing software applications that may use it.

Apart from insuring your computer system, steps you can take to protect your system include the following:

1. Run all of your computer equipment through a surge suppressor rather than directly through a wall outlet. Abrupt changes in electrical flow can instantly damage sensitive components and corrupt files. Surge suppressors ensure that the electrical flow to your system remains constant. If you're in an area that suffers frequent blackouts or brownouts, you should probably look into acquiring a unit that provides both surge suppression as well as back-up battery power.
2. Dust is another enemy. Keep your computer and printer covered when they are not being used, and store your floppy diskettes in enclosed cases.

3. Make two backup copies of all your software and important work files. Keep one set of the copies at your work site (where they'll be readily available if needed) and safely store the other set off site.
4. If you want to limit access to the computer, look for a system that's equipped with a lock to prevent it from being turned on without a key. Another option is to install password protection, which can be configured to allow specific individuals varying degrees of access to data residing on the computer. This allows you to keep sensitive information on the computer without fear of someone unauthorised reading it.
5. If download files off the Internet or an online service, get a programme that detects and removes computer viruses. Check all diskettes that you receive from others for viruses before you transfer the information on the diskettes to your computer. Also get in the habit of regularly running a virus check on your hard drive. Remember, it takes only one unchecked virus to cause a potentially devastating loss of both information and the use of your valuable computer equipment. Spyware is another growing threat that must be dealt with. Special software exists to help you block this sort of malware and to remove any examples that might find their way onto your hard drive before they can do any major damage.

6.3. LEASING YOUR EQUIPMENT

Nowadays, you should view leasing companies as potential suppliers for virtually all of your equipment and other tangible business assets. You should have little trouble finding companies willing to lease or rent motor vehicles, office furniture, store fixtures, computers, communications devices, manufacturing equipment, and other items you may need. The trick, of course, is determining when you would be better off leasing an asset instead of purchasing it.

The main advantage of leasing is that you can generally gain the use of an asset with less of an initial expenditure of cash than would be required if you purchased the asset. Equipment leases rarely require down payments. In other words, leasing may effectively provide the benefit of up to 100 percent financing (although a refundable security deposit may be required in some instances). In contrast, purchase loans frequently require down payments of up to 25 percent or more. If yours is a startup business that is strapped for cash or if you are finding it difficult to secure the credit necessary to finance your purchases, leasing may be your only real option for acquiring needed business assets.

Leases and rentals are contractual arrangements by which the owner of property (the "lessor") allows another person (the "lessee") to use the property for a stated period of time in exchange for cash payments or other compensation. There is no real legal distinction between a "lease" and a "rental." In practice, however, rentals generally are considered short-term arrangements, while leases are arrangements for longer terms (a year or more). The two main types of equipment leases you'll encounter are "true" leases and "financial" leases. You also may hear about "sales and leaseback" leases, which in reality are sophisticated financing transactions.

True leases: If the lessee acquires no rights to the property other than its use, then the lease is commonly referred to as a "true" (or "straight") lease. Under a true lease, the lessor is treated as the owner of the leased property for both tax and non-tax purposes, and the lessee's rental payments do not establish any equity in the property. A true lease usually gives the lessee the option to prematurely end the lease, subject to conditions that are spelled out in the agreement. If the lessor remains responsible for maintaining the property, then a true lease also may be referred to as an "operating" (or "maintenance") lease.

Financial leases: A lease that is used to effectively finance the purchase of assets is commonly referred to as a "financial" (or "financing" or "finance") lease. The distinguishing characteristics of financial leases are that (1) the duration of the lease generally coincides with the functional or economic life of the property, (2) the lease may not be cancelled, and (3) the lessee is responsible for maintaining the property. Frequently, a financial lease will be structured so that the lessee's only practical choice at the end of the lease is to purchase the asset. For accounting and tax purposes, financial leases are generally treated as a sale.

Sale and leaseback leases: Under a "sale and leaseback" arrangement, the owner of an asset sells the asset to a third party and then immediately leases it back. The benefit of this transaction is that the owner frees up the cash that was tied up in the asset (through the sale) while still retaining its use (through the leaseback). To a large extent, your expected need for the leased equipment will determine whether you end up with a true lease or a financial lease.

If you expect to need the equipment for most, if not all, of its useful life, then you'll probably end up with a financial lease. In contrast, if you expect that you'll need only the equipment for a specified period and that the equipment will be of use to someone else at the end of that period, you probably can find a lessor who's willing to set you up with a true lease arrangement.

Key lease terms. Here are some of the major terms commonly found in equipment leases of which you should be aware:

1. *Lease term*: Identifies how long the lease will be in effect. If you suspect that your need for the equipment may exceed the initial term, try negotiating the inclusion in the agreement of a renewal option that entitles you to renew the lease for a specified period or periods and for a specified rent.
2. *Rental rate*: Identifies how much the rent is and when it must be paid. Most leases also include late payment provisions that impose an additional charge if you fail to pay the rent when it's due or within a specified grace period. If your business experiences seasonal or irregular sales activity, try negotiating a flexible rental rate that corresponds to the changes in your cash flow.
3. *Maintenance*: Identifies who is required to maintain the equipment. Be wary about accepting a requirement that you provide a higher degree of maintenance than would be required if you owned the equipment.
4. *Improvements and modifications*: Identifies whether you have the right to make improvements or modifications to the equipment so that it better suits your needs. Depending on the equipment involved, you may want to specify who's responsible for modifications required by federal or state regulatory agencies.
5. *Insurance*: Identifies who is required to insure the equipment, as well as who is entitled to what part of any settlement if the equipment is lost, stolen, or damaged.
6. *Stipulated losses*: Specifies amounts you'll owe if the equipment is lost, stolen, or destroyed by casualty. Such amounts may be in addition to or in lieu of the value of the equipment.

7. *Purchase option*: Identifies whether you'll have the right or obligation to purchase the equipment. The provision should specify an option price or range and how and when the option may be exercised.
8. *Transfers*: Identifies whether you or the lessor has the right to transfer your respective interests in the lease. You want to be sure that a transfer by the lessor will in no way infringe upon your expectations under the lease. You'll also want to check under what conditions, if any, you'll be able to sublease the equipment to others.
9. *Claims*: Identifies whether you can sue and take other actions in the lessor's name to assert claims against suppliers and others with respect to the equipment and whether you're entitled to retain any settlements from such actions.
10. *Early termination and amendment*: Identifies under what conditions the lease may be amended or cancelled. These provisions become more important as the term of the lease increases. Try to forecast the circumstances under which the equipment may become uneconomical or useless to you, then try to negotiate a provision that addresses those circumstances.
11. *Modern equipment substitution*: Provides for updating the equipment or replacing it with a newer model during the lease term. This is an especially useful provision to have included in a lease for computer equipment, communications devices, and other items that are subject to rapid technological advancements.
12. *Termination costs*: Identifies who is responsible for the costs (dismantling, packing, shipping, insurance, etc.) related to returning equipment to the lessor at the end of the lease term.

13. *Master lease*: Identifies that additional equipment can be leased by an addendum to the agreement that describes the new equipment, the rental rate, and lease term. This type of provision can yield substantial savings in negotiation costs if you expect an ongoing relationship with the lessor.

6.4 LEASING vs. PURCHASING

The main advantage of leasing is that your initial outlay of cash to gain the use of an asset is generally less for leasing than it is for purchasing. However, perhaps the main disadvantage of leasing is that you usually end up paying out more over the asset's life than you would have paid if you purchased the asset. How do you reconcile these two factors? Well, one way is to do a mathematical analysis of your net cash flows that would result from leasing and from purchasing. A cash flow analysis provides an estimate of how much cash you would need to set aside today to cover the after-tax costs of each acquisition alternative.

Finding an equipment lessor shouldn't be too difficult. In addition to companies that specialise in leasing equipment, many of which are subsidiaries of banks, insurance companies, and finance companies, more and more manufacturers are now offering leasing plans. Check your local Yellow Pages, and you're sure to find a number of leads. To ensure that you'll have meaningful information to compare, provide each company with a written statement that details what you're after. This can go a long ways toward getting you quotes that are for the same equipment, have the same features, and are on the same terms.

Obviously, as you compare quotes, you're going to pay careful attention to how much rent each company is proposing to charge. However, you'll also do well to look into the each company's reputation for dealing with its lessees. Most equipment leases will bind you into a relationship for a number of years, so you want to be sure that your lessor is going to treat you fairly and be responsive to your needs. If possible, get references from former and present customers of the company.

Once you have a quote that you feel is worth pursuing from a reputable company, you need to reach a formal agreement on a lease with the company. Depending on your bargaining position, you may or may not be able to negotiate changes to the company's standard lease agreement. However, it generally doesn't hurt to ask, so if there's a provision in the agreement that you're uncomfortable with or if you have a provision you'd like to see added, make your concerns known. In any event, do not sign the lease until you are comfortable that you fully understand all of its terms.

If the lease involves a significant commitment on your part, either in money or in time, have your attorney review it and advise you on any of its potentially adverse provisions. If you're going to invest your precious capital in purchasing equipment, you want to be sure that you do all you can to get the best deals for your money. You can go a long ways toward achieving this goal by simply taking the time to comparison shop.

As you shop around for equipment deals, don't overlook the used equipment market. Depending on the item, you may be able to purchase used equipment for a fraction of what you would have paid if the equipment were new and without any loss of functionality. Purchasing used office furnishings, in particular, can lead to big savings. Where can you find high-quality used equipment? Start by checking the Yellow Pages for listings of thrift stores and second-hand dealers.

Be especially watchful for ads mentioning sales related to an office re-modelling or business liquidation. And as more people get into — and sometimes out of — home businesses, yard and estate sales may also provide bargains to those with the time and patience to seek them out. Occasionally, you may come across used equipment that is still covered by an original warranty or service agreement. However, before you take comfort in the potential protection such an agreement may provide, read through it to confirm that its benefits are in fact transferable to you with the equipment

Unless you're in the position of having had a vendor immediately agree to sell you the specific equipment you want for the price you're willing to pay, you're going to have to negotiate. If you've gone through the initial exercise of determining what you want and need and what you're willing to pay for the equipment and its various features, you'll have a head start on the process. This is because you'll have an idea as to which features or conditions are most important to you and which you may be willing to concede to reach an acceptable compromise.

At the very least, establish in your mind what your minimum requirements are, and be prepared to walk away if you're not comfortable that the deal being offered will meet your needs. As you proceed to negotiate your best deal, try to be fair and cordial. Especially if you expect to have future dealings with the vendor, whether in connection with your use or the servicing of the equipment or with future purchases, you don't want to push so hard that you end up souring your business relationship. Even if a vendor starts with an offer that sounds acceptable, you won't lose anything by at least trying for an improvement in price or terms. Given that most everything in business is negotiable to some degree, simply inquiring whether the offer is the best the vendor can do may lead to some pleasantly surprising results.

Unless your business has unlimited cash reserves, chances are that at some point you're going to have to finance an equipment purchase. In fact, even equipment that you purchase for cash is in one sense financed, if you end up borrowing to meet other needs because the purchase depleted your working capital. So, you really should view equipment financing as just one piece of your overall financing strategy for your business. If you anticipate financing an equipment purchase, compare the credit packages offered by your bank, independent financing companies, and the equipment's manufacturer and vendors. These packages can vary greatly in terms of down-payment amounts, interest rates, loan durations, security requirements, late payment charges, and similar provisions.

With respect to security requirements, make sure you understand what each package will require as collateral. Will the financed equipment be the only collateral or will you be required to put up other assets as well? If you must put up other assets as collateral, check your existing financing agreements to ensure they don't contain any restrictions on your ability to encumber those assets. Apart from collateral requirements, carefully review any restrictions that the lender may propose to place on your operations.

6.5. USING PERSONAL ASSETS FOR BUSINESS

As you explore your options for equipping your business, don't overlook the possibility of using items that you already own. Putting items such as your cars, office furnishings, and computer equipment to work in your business, even if only on a temporary basis, can free up dollars that you would have otherwise spent on acquisition costs. Furthermore, you'll enjoy the tax benefit of claiming depreciation deductions with respect to the items that you convert to business use. If you're conducting business as a sole proprietorship, there's really no trick to converting your personal assets.

All it takes is to start using them in your business. Perhaps your only real concern will be confirming whether you'll lose insurance coverage for the converted items under your homeowners policy. If so, you'll want to be sure to have the items covered by your business policy. For depreciation purposes, you'll need to know both the amount that you originally paid for each converted item and the fair market value at the time you started using it for business because your deductions must be computed on the basis of the lower of those two amounts.

7

HOW TO USE MY OFFICE EQUIPMENT

There is no one right way to design and equip a workspace. What works for someone else may not work for you. A word about organising your business records and supplies: although you need to be comfortable with any system that you create, this doesn't mean that you're locked into organising your business the same way you handle your personal records. Your business gives you a fresh start. If you haven't approached your personal recordkeeping with the care that it deserves, you have a second chance to do things differently in your business.

Getting productivity out of your equipment is a bit different from using equipment efficiently, which is more concerned with saving you time and money. Frequently you must balance time and cost considerations against how they will affect your equipment's ability to function. For example, think about a fax machine. You can probably operate such a machine at a lower cost if you use a single phone line for both phone and fax transmissions. But if you need to send or receive faxes at the same time you're making phone calls, the fax machine won't be able to do its job. To use the fax productively in that situation, you may have to maintain a second phone line.

Take the time to ask yourself a few questions about what you do and how your equipment helps you to do it. Some questions you should ask include:

1. Are you dealing with the public or is the office primarily for your private use?
2. Which pieces of equipment do you use most frequently to do your job?
3. How much electrical power and how many outlets does your equipment require?
4. Do you have a significant amount of paper to keep track of, or keep filed?
5. Do you need a large desk surface to do your work (for example, for drafting)?
6. Does your work require you to frequently consult reference manuals or other books?

If you know that you must consult price catalogues regularly, don't put the bookshelf in which you store them in your attic to make room for a nice looking potted tree that you can't use to get the job done. If you do, you could be tempted to refrain from trudging upstairs to consult the catalogues and, instead, rely on your memory for the price of a dozen widgets — with disastrous results. Consider how systems will work together. Remember what happened when you were trying to watch The Flintstones as a kid and your mom started to vacuum in the next room? The buzzing lines that filled your television screen demonstrated that two pieces of equipment may be useful by themselves but not work well together.

This problem is also evident in the example of the fax machine that is receiving an incoming transmission on the same telephone line that you need in order to make an important sales call. System conflicts that should be avoided with careful planning include:

1. *Power availability problems*: Consider the effect of supplemental heating and air conditioning units on power availability when the weather starts changing. Some equipment may also distort radio transmissions or cause static on a cordless phone.
2. *Temperature discrepancies*: Be wary of placing equipment that generates heat (for example, a photocopier) or magnetic fields too close to computer disks and other sensitive equipment.
3. *Lighting conditions*: Many people working on a computer terminal like things darker to minimise screen glare. The same darkness causes problems for both solar powered devices and your eyes, if you're trying to read. Arrange lights so that you can turn some off when you are working onscreen and turn others on when you are working at your desk.
4. *Infrared system failures*: There's much talk today about the wireless office. Some systems send data over the airwaves to a printer or fax machine in the corner. Will putting two of these machines in the same room cause a problem? Will such a machine interfere with a burglar alarm system? Plan accordingly.
5. *Rolling office chairs and carpeting*: They may generate static electricity harmful to computer components.
6. *Noisy equipment*: It can render the dictation tape you prepared for your transcriptionist — or worse, the phone message you left for an important client — unintelligible.

7.1. SETTING UP EQUIPMENT EFFICIENTLY

Two key factors determine whether equipment is being used efficiently. The first is time, the second is money.

Unless your office equipment's layout helps you to save both time and money, it is not efficient. As you strive for efficiency, however, be sure that you don't compromise your equipment's productivity. Can you plan business meetings with clients, call them, draft proposals for them, and get projects "off the ground" from your desk chair? Here are some tips that can help:

1. Avoid using built-in desks and other furniture if possible. Movable equipment can be rearranged as your workflow changes. For similar reasons an adjustable chair is useful.
2. Use adjustable shelving if possible. If it turns out that you use a tall, fat book most, you won't have to store it on a shelf that's hard to reach just because it is the only place where the book fits.
3. Avoid placing equipment and supplies where you'll have to move them again in order to use other equipment or supplies. You shouldn't have to move two boxes of envelopes to get to a box of letterhead stationery.
4. Organise filing systems so that you will handle a piece of paper only once before it goes where it belongs.
5. Don't forget that computer applications are work tools too. Be sure to organise computer programmes so that the ones you use most can be accessed easily from your programme manager.
6. Unless clients regularly visit your office, the efficiency of your system is probably more important than how it looks.

Everyone in business wants to save money, and in the case of a small business, protecting your cash flow is vital. Proper arrangement and use of your equipment can help you do this. Here are some tips:

1. Consider the abilities of machines that do more than one thing. Manufacturers now cram multiple features into their equipment. Take advantage of these features to streamline your workflow and save on supplies. For example, you may be able to cut down on fax paper and toner expenses — and you won't have to leave your desk — if you use your computer to send and receive messages when you don't need a paper copy.
2. Consider the limits of machines that do more than one thing. Fax machines double as telephones, photocopiers, printers, and even scanners. Although using a fax machine to make a copy once in a while shouldn't be a problem, if you are making a high volume of copies on it, you may wear it out much faster. Moreover, you'll probably go through supplies that are much more expensive than what a desktop copier would consume.
3. Put equipment where you can take advantage of natural lighting from windows. This may enable you to use fewer lights at lower wattage.
4. Don't place your equipment where it will be subjected to environmental hazards such as extreme heat and cold. Heavy dust can also cause extreme damage to delicate equipment like computers. This is especially important to think about when you put your home office in a garage, attic, or cellar.
5. Remember that your time is worth money. Any system that helps you to work faster saves money if it frees you to work on other matters that help to generate profits.

7.2. SETTING UP A COMFORTABLE OFFICE

In home offices and small offices where a computer is used frequently, an improperly arranged workstation can be a source of major discomfort. In fact, the Occupational Safety and Hazards Administration now studies office and computer ergonomics and is concerned with the consequences of long-term exposure to poorly designed environments. They can contribute to such physical ailments as general fatigue, irritated eyes, and soreness or pain in the wrists, neck, shoulders, legs, and back. To help alleviate these problems, you should look into acquiring an adjustable computer desk and chair that allows you to:

1. Position the keyboard at elbow height so that you can work it with your wrists remaining straight and with your elbows maintaining a 90 degree angle.
2. Position the monitor so that the top of the screen is right at or slightly below eye level.
3. Sit with your feet flat on the floor, your knees at a 90 degree angle, your back against the chair back, and your hips at a slightly obtuse (greater than 90 degree) angle. Position the monitor so that the top of the screen is right at or slightly below eye level.

To further combat eye fatigue, try setting your monitor's contrast to high and its brightness to low. Also, try to keep the screen free of dust and smudges. If glare from overhead lights or windows is reflecting off the screen, try tilting the monitor slightly downward or using an antiglare screen or hood. No matter how well your workstation is arranged, you're going to experience some soreness or pains if you don't take occasional breaks from your work at the computer. Force yourself to take a few minutes each hour to stand up and stretch, to move around, or to focus your view on an object that's across the room.

One thing that can make a small office very uncomfortable is unwanted noise. In some cases you may want to move particularly noisy equipment outside of your office, as long as it won't compromise productivity or efficiency. Heavy carpeting and drapes may also help to absorb noise. Moreover, a rubber mat placed beneath a machine may help to keep it from vibrating loudly.

7.3. PROTECTING YOUR EQUIPMENT

Once you've committed your valuable time and money to acquiring equipment for your business, the last thing you need is to have the equipment damaged or destroyed (whether by accidents or acts of nature) stolen, or lost. In a very real sense, your equipment represents relatively long-term investments that you have made in your business. And, just like any other investments you make, the economic investment in your equipment needs to be protected from significant risks. Such protection can take two forms: protecting the equipment itself (such as by security and fire-protection measures) and protecting the value of the equipment by obtaining insurance.

Keep an equipment inventory: A good first step in protecting your investment in equipment is to maintain an accurate and up-to-date listing of what you own. For each item that you acquire, record on a master list the acquisition date, the vendor's name, a description of the item (including its brand name and serial number, if any), and the item's cost. It also doesn't hurt to supplement the list with a photograph of each item and copies of your receipts. This type of record keeping could prove to be invaluable in identifying your losses should a major catastrophe or theft hit your business. You should also use the list to take occasional inventories of your equipment to ensure that all items are present. Keep the list (and photographs and receipts) in a safe place, with at least one copy stored off site.

Anti-theft procedures: As an anti-theft measure, consider using an engraving tool or other means to mark each item that's capable of being stolen with an easily seen identification number and with your or your business's name. Also, try to keep smaller items of value locked up, or at least out of sight, when they're not being used. Of course, part and parcel with protecting your equipment is taking steps to secure your facility as a whole.

Finally, it almost goes without saying that you should get property insurance if you have a significant investment in your equipment.

7.3.1. Property Insurance

In shopping for property insurance for your equipment, look for a policy that's written on an "all-risks" basis as opposed to on a "named-peril" basis. An all-risk policy generally provides coverage for all risks or perils, excepting only those that the policy specifically identifies. In contrast, a named-peril policy covers only the specific risks and perils that the policy identifies. In theory, you may require a number of named-peril policies to provide the same scope of coverage offered by a single all-risk policy. For this reason, an all-risk policy reduces the chance that you'll have gaps in coverage or duplication of coverage. If you should decide to go with an all-risk policy, carefully review the enumerated exclusions. For those exclusions that you believe create an unacceptable risk to your business, try to get coverage on a named-peril basis.

7.4. REPLACING EQUIPMENT

Very few items of equipment, if any, have an infinite working life. Well, maybe you could expect a paperclip to last forever, but then again it would probably get lost at some point. Accordingly, you can generally assume that the equipment that you use in your business is going to break down eventually. This, in turn, will require you to decide whether you should repair or replace the equipment. You may also face an equipment replacement decision whenever newer models or makes of your current equipment arrive on the market.

In many respects, the repair-or-replace decision is similar to the decision of whether to acquire a given item of equipment in the first place. The first question you should probably ask yourself is whether your business in fact still needs the equipment that you're thinking about repairing or replacing. Will the repaired or replacement equipment make your business more profitable, efficient, or productive? If not, perhaps you should just consider the existing asset to be unproductive and eliminate it.

How then should you determine the proper course of action? Well, a thorough cost-benefit analysis of each of your options might prove useful. For example, if you were trying to determine whether to repair or replace a broken item, you would compare the costs and associated benefits of repairing the item versus the costs and associated benefits of replacing it. In some cases, however, factors outside the straight economic analysis of costs and benefits will (and should) drive your decision.

For example, you may conclude that you just can't afford the potential downtimes associated with your older equipment breaking down, so you choose to replace the equipment, even though your direct repair costs would be minimal. Or, your concerns about the health and safety of you and your employees may lead you to replace an existing item with a newer, safer model, even though it's unlikely that you'll realise any increased revenues or cost savings from using the newer equipment.

7.5. DISPOSING THE UNWANTED EQUIPMENT

Every item of equipment that you acquire for your business represents an investment of your business capital. Taken a step further, an item that is not currently being used represents capital on which the current return to your business is zero or even negative (if property taxes and insurance costs attributable to the item are taken into account). For this reason, you want to be sure to limit the amount of unproductive assets that your business owns. Adopt a practice of taking regular inventories of all of your equipment to confirm each item's current level of use.

If you come across an item that you're currently not using, try to determine whether you have a definite future use for the item that justifies the continuing cost of holding it. If you don't foresee such a future use, seriously consider selling or otherwise disposing of the item. If you're unable to sell an unproductive item of equipment, or to use it as a trade-in on the purchase of an item you need, you may be able to generate a tax deduction by donating the item to charity or by simply abandoning (junking) it.

8
HOW TO MAINTAIN THE SECURITY OF MY OFFICE

The security of your workplace, your property, and, to a lesser degree, the security of your employees' property are responsibilities you cannot afford to overlook. The costs, both in dollars and peace of mind, can be staggering when you find that you've been "ripped off." Concern yourself with:

1. Burglary prevention.
2. Embezzlement prevention.
3. Security policies.

8.1. BURGLARY PREVENTION

Protecting your office and equipment as well as your employees' property from vandals and thieves should be an important part of your safety programme. There are a many ways to safeguard your business, including the use of locks, key control, lighting, and alarm systems.

Locks: Use of dead bolt locks, where appropriate, and the use of double cylinder dead locks, requiring that a key be used to open the door from either side, can go a long way in discouraging burglary of tempting theft targets. Additionally, you can get some discounts from your insurer when you are adequately locked-up. But locks don't help if you don't remember to use them. Be sure all doors and windows have locks and that those locks are sturdy and, above all, used. Get into the habit of checking all the doors and windows before you lock up and leave for the night. Don't assume that because a door was locked yesterday — and because you didn't see anyone use the door — it is still locked. Be safe rather than sorry.

Key control: After proper locks are installed, key control is also essential to making sure that the property remains secure. To make sure keys don't fall into the wrong hands:

1. Issue as few keys as possible.
2. Establish specific rules regarding the "loaning-out" of keys by those to whom they are issued.
3. Take a periodic inventory of keys.
4. Get keys that say "do not duplicate."
5. Control who can make duplicate keys.

Remember, too, that locks aren't just for doors. There are window locks, desk locks, file cabinet locks, and even computer hard drive locks. Make sure you have keys and key control for all of them.

Good lighting: Lighting, both indoor and outdoor, can be of great assistance in burglary prevention. Darkness hides burglars and makes their work easy. If you are trying to decide whether to light an area, compare the expense of lighting the area with what you'll lose if you are vandalised.

Alarms: Burglar alarms, either silent or with a siren or bell, should also be used as part of any burglary prevention programme. In deciding which type of system is best for your business, decide first whether you want to catch the intruder inside or outside your premises. Since there are several types of alarm systems on the market today, do your homework before buying a system and evaluate several systems' benefits and drawbacks.

8.2. EMBEZZLEMENT PREVENTION

Embezzlement has been defined as "the fraudulent appropriation of property by a person to whom it has been entrusted." Embezzlement doesn't happen only to Fortune 500 firms. It happens every day to the small business owner. Small businesses are less likely to take the precautions necessary to prevent embezzlement. The best ways to combat embezzlement are to:

1. Recognise the warning signs.
2. Establish internal audit controls.
3. Bond employees.

Here are some warning signs that embezzlement is taking place:

1. Increase in overall sales returns might represent a concealment of accounts receivable payments.
2. Unusual bad-debt write-offs could be covering up a fraudulent scheme; a decline or unusually small increase in cash or credit sales could mean that some sales are not being recorded.
3. Bounced business checks could indicate that funds are being siphoned out of your bank account.
4. Inventory shortages could indicate fictitious purchases, unrecorded sales, or employee pilferage.
5. Profit declines and increases in expenses could be a sign that cash is being siphoned off illegitimately.
6. Slow collections can be a device to mask embezzlement.

There are four basic things that you can do in implementing an internal system of controls:

1. Screen applicants before they are hired.
2. Periodically examine cancelled checks to see if there is anything unusual.
3. Take precautions in preparing payroll: have more than one person prepare it, have several different people prepare it, or oversee it yourself.
4. Have two people sign off on checks, preferably in front of each other.

While there is no foolproof system of accounting or internal control that will absolutely prevent employee dishonesty losses, an environment can be created where employee pilfering is discouraged. The first step is to review every area where potential dishonesty problems could arise, including:

1. Inventory control.
2. Data processing.
3. Purchasing.
4. Receiving.
5. Bookkeeping.
6. Cash disbursements.

In setting up an internal audit system, it's common procedurally for most companies to divide financial responsibilities and functions so that no one employee controls all aspects of a transaction. Hence, insurers and consultants recommend the following:

1. Require checks to be countersigned by two responsible officials.
2. Limit the endorsement of checks, by anyone other than the owner, to deposits for credit only.

3. Delegate the responsibility for receiving checks and cash to someone other than the person who records incoming funds.
4. Mail statements to outside accounts directly at least monthly.
5. Examine payroll records periodically to prevent padding.
6. Make sure that employees responsible for ordering goods and supplies are not the same ones responsible for receiving them or paying for them.
7. Do not give the person who has the authority to write off bad debts the authority to make a credit sale or loan.
8. If someone else does payroll, make sure you have access to payroll data on the computer and that no one changes the passwords or access requirements for that data.

Dividing financial responsibilities and functions is not enough, though. Take an inventory of your merchandise at least annually and have an outside public accountant audit your cash and accounts annually.

8.2.1. Bonding Process

Even if you have an internal auditing system that makes embezzlement difficult, the danger of collusion still exists. Consequently, some companies protect themselves from employee dishonesty by bonding their employees. Bonding, the process by which an employer can be indemnified for the loss of money or other property sustained through dishonest acts of a "bonded" employee, can cover many types of acts including larceny, theft, embezzlement, forgery, misappropriation, wrongful abstraction, willful misapplication, or other fraudulent or dishonest acts committed by an employee, alone or in collusion with others.

There are several types of fidelity bonds. Discuss each with your agent to determine whether damages from negligence are covered. Basically, your business has several options at its disposal, which are:

- — Individual — covers one employee (usually purchased by small concerns or family-operated businesses with only one employee).
- — Name schedule or position schedule — covers either the employees or positions specified.
- — Blanket fidelity — covers all employees.
- — Commercial, blanket, and blanket position — provides multiple protection (comprehensive dishonesty, disappearance, and destruction coverage, or a blanket crime policy).

8.3. SECURITY POLICY

As part of your security programme, you should write security rules and give them to your employees. You may want to include your security rules in your employee handbook, if you have one. What should you include in your policy? Security is a broad issue, and you may choose to keep the focus of your policy narrow, or you may choose to address many different aspects of security in your policy. Some topics that you might include are:

- — Guards and security.
- — Your security programme/committee.
- — Areas of limited access.
- — Restrictions on visitors.
- — Statements regarding the removal of company property.

— Escort services to cars, if you provide it.

8.4. RECOVERY PLANNING FOR DISASTER

It seems lately that natural disasters are occurring with more frequency and intensity. In the past few years, in particular, floods, earthquakes, fires, mudslides, tornadoes, and hurricanes have caused millions of dollars in damages to the homes and businesses they strike. While you can't prevent a natural disaster from occurring, you can help minimise its impact on your business by being prepared if disaster strikes.

Think you don't need to worry? Ask yourself — can all or part of your worksite cease to exist for one day or permanently? Would you survive the financial disaster? If the answer is probably not, it underscores how important fire, disaster recovery, and contingency planning are. The following sample plans assume that all or a part of your business has ceased to exist in the location it is in for a period of time. How you continue and recreate your business are the goals of these plans.

If you have trouble getting motivated to do it, think of how much better shape your business will be in if you do. After a disaster occurs, you may be the only business of your kind standing and ready to go. Think of how much business you could do! Each business's plan is unique, yet the process of developing the plan has many similarities. To help prepare for a disaster, take the following steps:

— Develop a contingency plan.

— Develop emergency procedures.

8.4.1. Contingency Plan

Think of your contingency plan as a fire drill. While you may never have a fire, it's good to know what to do if there is one. Approach general contingency planning the same way. Use these steps to get started:

— *Get organised*: Establish a task force composed of a few employees, if you have them. If you choose not to lead the charge, name a key person with authority to get the plan done. Support that plan.

— *Assume the worst*: Assume that the physical facility that houses the business and all of its contents has been permanently destroyed. From that scenario, list each item that would be important to the business if salvaged and what must be recreated from scratch in order to continue. Typically, the most critical items are business records. Furniture, materials, and manuals usually can be replaced and are insured for their value.

— *Try to prevent the loss*: Of those items on the list that should be salvaged, or must be recreated, determine if there are any alternatives that could have been pursued before the disaster to avoid a total loss. Alternatives may include:

  — Keeping duplicate records at a different site.

  — Keeping backup equipment necessary to continue basic operations at a location other than the worksite (perhaps a storage facility or, in the case of computer equipment, in your home).

  — Storing tapes of critical information such as accounts receivable, client information, or outstanding billings in a safe and secure place such as a bank vault.

— *Sweat the small stuff*: In addition to planning alternatives, you should include the following in your plans:

- — Determine the adequacy of fire and disaster insurance.
- — Complete emergency evacuation planning, including periodic drills, emergency plans, special considerations for any employees with disabilities, and coordination with local emergency and fire authorities.
- — Establish a plan for an alternate work site during the emergency, including records, staff, and support such as telephone, equipment, and related support.
- — Specify under what circumstances a facility will be closed (such as bad weather), who makes the decision, how the decision is communicated, and whether the employees are compensated.
- — If your company operates 24 hours a day or provides a critical service, determine the plan for alternative electricity, water storage, and other routine public services.
- — Plan a public relations spokesperson's responsibilities carefully and thoroughly (usually, that means you).
- — Have individuals with key responsibilities keep copies of the emergency plan at their homes in the event of an emergency.
- — Update the plan at least annually.
- — Determine if there are any local (usually industry-specific) groups that offer consulting, training, and reciprocal support in the area of disaster planning.

— *Train any employees periodically on fire prevention*: There should be a minimum of two fire drills a year and frequent on-site self inspection and review.

— Train at least one employee in emergency medical steps (such as CPR).

8.4.2. Emergency Procedures

If you have any employees, post instructions in the work areas concerning what to do in case of a fire, earthquake, or other disaster and make sure that your employees are familiar with those instructions. You should also be sure to have at least one smoke alarm and fire extinguisher in the work area. You may also consider having occasional fire drills to make sure employees know what to do. Even the best laid plans should have provisions for when all else fails. The most important thing to remember is that you don't have to go through the recovery process alone (even though it may feel like that to you at the time). In addition to various state and local economic development programmes, the federal government offers relief to disaster victims, including small business owners, through various sources.

9

KEEPING THE SAFETY OF MY WORKPLACE

Both humanitarian desires and economic good sense have encouraged employers to create and maintain safer and healthier working conditions. Where employers have not gone far enough, employees, unions, and government agencies have applied pressure for greater efforts.

9.1. NEED OF SAFETY PROGRAMME

Your plan should consider your company's immediate needs and provide for on-going, long-lasting worker protection. Once your plan is designed, it is important to follow through and use it in the workplace. You will then have a programme to anticipate, identify, and eliminate conditions or practices that could result in injuries and illnesses. If you have difficulty in deciding where to begin, a phone call to your state consultation programme (or the services of a private consultant) will get you the assistance you need.

You should continue to be governed by the policies, plans, and procedures you have established. In the event that you feel you have a conflict between the various laws, seek advice from an experienced attorney or consultant. Some of the steps in the process include:

1. Analysing your workplace.
2. Involving your employees in creating a programme.
3. Training supervisors and employees.
4. Implementing your safety programme.
5. Documenting your programme and writing a safety policy.

Basically, you need to concern yourself with the types of accidents and health hazard exposures that could happen in your workplace. Because each workplace is unique, your programme will differ from that of your neighbour or competitor.

9.2. WORKSITE ANALYSIS

It is your responsibility to know what you have in your workplace that could hurt your workers. Worksite analysis is a group of processes that helps you make sure that you know what you need to keep your workers safe. You may need help in getting started with these processes. Gather specific facts about your situation. Before you make any changes in your safety and health operations, you will want to gather as much information as possible about the current conditions at your workplace and about business practices that are already part of your safety and health programme. This information can help you identify any workplace problems and see what's involved in solving them.

The assessment of your workplace should be conducted by the person responsible for the safety and health programme and/or a professional safety and health consultant.

1. Request a consultation visit covering both safety and health to get a full survey of the hazards that exist in your workplace and those that could develop.

2. Establish a system, such as vendor consultations, to get expert help when you make changes and to be sure that the changes are not introducing new hazards into your workplace. Also, find ways, such as through trade groups, to keep current on newly recognised hazards in your industry.
3. Make a commitment to look carefully at each type of job done in your workplace from time to time, taking it apart step-by-step to see if there are any hidden hazards in the equipment or procedures. Some initial instructions from a consultant may be necessary.
4. Set up a system of checking to make sure that your hazard controls haven't failed and that new hazards haven't appeared. This is usually done by routine self-inspections.
5. Provide a way for your employees to let you know when they see things that look harmful to them and encourage them to use the process.
6. Learn how to do a thorough investigation when things do go wrong and someone gets sick or hurt. This will help you find ways to prevent recurrences.
7. If you've been in business for a while, take the time to look back over several years of injury or illness experience to identify patterns that can lead to more effective prevention. Thereafter, periodically look back over several months of experience to determine if any new patterns are developing.

Once you know what your hazards and potential hazards are, you are ready to put in place the systems that prevent or control those hazards. Your state or private consultant can help you do this. Whenever possible, you will want to eliminate those hazards. Sometimes that can be done through substitution of a less toxic material or through engineering controls that can be built in. When you cannot eliminate hazards, systems should be set up to control them. Here are some actions to take:

1. Set up safe work procedures, based on the analysis of the hazards in your employees' jobs, and make sure that employees understand the job procedures and follow them. This may be easier if employees are involved in the analysis that results in those procedures.
2. Be ready, if necessary, to enforce the rules for safe work procedures by asking your employees to help you set up a disciplinary system that will be fair and understood by everyone.
3. Where necessary to protect your employees, provide, at your own cost, personal protective equipment (PPE) according to published standards and be sure that your employees know why they need it, how to use it, and how to maintain it.
4. Provide for regular equipment maintenance to prevent breakdowns that can create hazards.
5. Plan for emergencies, including fire and natural disasters, and drill everyone frequently so that if the real thing happens, everyone will know what to do, even under stressful conditions.
6. You must ensure the ready availability of medical personnel for advice and consultation on matters of employee health. This does not mean that you must provide health care. But if health problems develop in your workplace, you are expected to get medical help to treat them and their causes.

To fulfil the above requirements, consider the following:

1. Have an emergency medical procedure for handling injuries, transporting ill or injured workers, and notifying medical facilities with a

minimum of confusion. Posting emergency numbers is a good idea.

2. Survey the medical facilities near your place of business and make arrangements for them to handle routine and emergency cases. Cooperative agreements could possibly be made with nearby plants that have medical personnel or facilities on-site.
3. If your business is remote from medical facilities, you are required to ensure that a person or persons be adequately trained and available to render first aid. Adequate first aid supplies must be readily available for emergency use.

An effective accident prevention programme requires proper job performance from everyone in the workplace. As a business owner, you must ensure that all employees know about the materials and equipment they work with, what known hazards are in the operation, and how you are controlling the hazards. Each employee needs to know the following:

1. No employee is expected to undertake a job until he or she has received job instructions on how to do it properly and has been authorised to perform that job.
2. No employee should undertake a job that appears unsafe.
3. Consider combining safety and health training with other training that you do, depending upon the potential and existing hazards that you have. Your training goal is that all employees know how to keep themselves and their fellow workers safe and healthy.

Here are some actions to take:

1. Ask your state or private consultant to recommend training for your worksite. The consultant may be

able to do some of the training while he or she is there.

2. Industry groups, trade periodicals, and other similar sources are ways to discover additional training resources.
3. Make sure that you have trained your employees on every potential hazard that they could be exposed to and how to protect themselves. Then verify that they really understand what you taught them.
4. Pay particular attention to your new employees and to tenured employees who are moving to new jobs. Because they are learning new operations, they are more likely to get hurt.
5. Employees who are having personal problems may also need special attention. Make sure that you train your supervisors to know all the hazards that face the people they supervise and how to reinforce training with quick reminders and refreshers, and with disciplinary action if necessary. Verify that they know what is expected of them.

— Make sure that you and your top management staff understand all of your responsibilities and how to hold subordinate supervisory employees accountable for their responsibilities.

9.3. IMPLEMENTATION OF SAFETY PROGRAMME

Here are some things to take into consideration when implementing your safety programme. Have an insurance plan. You will need an insurance plan. Beyond the liability protection you will receive, don't expect much more from insurers. Their goals are different from yours; hence, they may not have the in-depth expertise to provide many of the services you may need concerning training, noise surveys, engineering services, and industrial hygiene.

Don't dwell on your programme's structure and reporting relationships. It really does not matter to whom one reports within your business. Promote a safe workplace. The best claim is the one that never happened. The primary policy of each employer should be to avoid accidents in the first place. How can you accomplish this seemingly impossible task? Avoiding accidents can be simple, such as ensuring that employees use safety equipment, or difficult, such as restructuring job tasks and duties in a more ergonomically efficient way.

One important part of the on-going administration of your safety programme and efforts is documentation. Document your activities in all elements of your workplace programme. Essential records, including those legally required for workers' compensation, insurance audits, and government inspections, must be maintained as long as the actual need exists. Keeping records of your activities, such as policy statements, training sessions for management and employee safety and health meetings held, information distributed to employees, and medical arrangements made, is also a smart idea.

A written safety policy is the beginning of any safety programme. The policy statement sets the tone and indicates what the consequences will be. It does not have to be elaborate, but a written policy should reflect the following:

1. The purpose of the safety programme.
2. Who will be assigned safety responsibilities and what their responsibilities and accountability requirements will be.

Begin by analysing past accidents or safety problems — if they happened before and they were not corrected, they will happen again. Next, look at your industry as a whole and then look at OSHA (OSHA is the federal agency that enforces federal safety requirements) standards. There are specific statements and elements your safety policy should contain. They will help to not only reflect your philosophy and the intent of your safety policy, but also give specific information and guidance to employees about safety. Your policy should contain:

1. A strongly worded affirmative statement that acknowledges and supports the company's responsibility
2. Titles, positions, and locations of those responsible for policy design, enforcement, and modification
3. A system for any employee to report violations of safety rules confidentially
4. Documentation that establishes that the policy was given to all employees, posted prominently, and included in policy manuals
5. A statement that supervisors are held to act as agents for the company
6. A statement that any deviation from known policy by supervisors will not be tolerated
7. A process to address how questions are to be answered and emergencies handled
8. The penalties for employees who don't follow safety rules

Having a policy doesn't mean that you've done enough to ensure safety. Make sure that your policy is understood and followed. To protect yourself, you'll also want to document that you have shared your policy and enforced it, in the event of an accident. Follow these guidelines to make sure that your policy is implemented and applied:

1. All employees should sign a document stating that they have read, understood, and will follow the company policy.
2. The signed document should be retained in the employee's personnel file.
3. New employees should sign prior to actual work.
4. As the policy is updated, new sign-offs should be secured.
5. Safety training should be provided for supervisors and employees.
6. Safety bulletins and other communications should be distributed as information changes.
7. Discipline should be consistently applied to all individuals in similar circumstances.
8. Supervisors should be fully advised of the impact of their actions, given special caution concerning sole reliance on verbal instructions for safety directions, and urged to provide closer supervision to workers who are known to have violated safety rules or have personal problems that may interfere with their attention to their work.
9. As requested or scheduled, supervisors should perform independent inspections and follow up inspections to ensure the work areas and employees are conforming to safety rules.

9.4. SAFETY ISSUES

As the workplace becomes a more dangerous place and as we learn more about hazards, new safety issues and concerns emerge. In some cases, OSHA is taking action, or is considering taking action, to address some of these newer workplace hazards.

9.4.1. Office Automation Hazards

People may tend to think that safety in the workplace is an issue that needs to be addressed only by companies that perform "dangerous" work such as foundries, steel mills, and auto manufacturers. But that's not true. Today's modern office is full of potential hazards that both you and your employees need to be aware of and for which you need to take appropriate precautions.

For example, cloth and vinyl chairs, carpeting and drapery, and the large quantity of paper found in many offices can create a fire hazard. Misplaced waste baskets, poorly lighted halls, substances tracked in from outside that may cause people to slip, frayed carpet, a file drawer left open, telephone and electrical cords on the floor, and office machines being used by those who do not know how to use them are other examples of office safety hazards. With the dramatic increase in office automation, a primary source of injuries in the office may not be from movement — such as lifting heaving objects or running into things — but from a lack of movement.

Office automation encourages people to sit in one place for long periods of time. To combat injuries and illness related to office work, you need to have an understanding of:

— Ergonomics.

— Illnesses and injuries caused by office work.

— Preventing office automation-related illness and injuries.

9.4.1.1. Ergonomics

Ergonomics is the study of the spatial design of job requirements and worksites in relation to human physical and psychological capabilities and limitations. Two major ergonomic considerations are the physical interaction of your employees with equipment they use on the job and the range of motion that employees have in doing their jobs.

For example, if your employees work in front of a computer all day, you'll want to make sure that their chairs are at the proper height to allow them to reach the keyboard while maintaining good posture. You'll also want to make sure that their faces are not too close to the keyboard so that their vision is not damaged by sitting too close to the monitor. Also, if your employees have to do a great deal of typing or filing or other tasks that require that they maintain the same position or repeat the same physical motions for a long time, you'll want to make sure that they receive ample opportunity to stretch and possibly vary their tasks to avoid physical injury from the repetitive motion.

9.4.1.2. Illnesses and injuries

Just as the hazards of the office are different from the industrial workplace, so are the injuries that can result.

Repetitive motion injuries: Also known as cumulative trauma disorders (CTDs), these are injuries that build slowly over time to the point of becoming a painful injury to an employee. They occur when an employee performs the same task in the same range of motion over a long period of time without taking proper precautions to make sure that no injury occurs. The most common cumulative trauma disorder is known as carpal tunnel syndrome, and it is a painful injury that can debilitate the hands, wrists, and arms of an employee.

Carpal tunnel syndrome stems primarily from the repetitive motions of typing and computer work. In carpal tunnel syndrome, the frequent bending of the wrist causes tendons or tissue to swell in the tunnel formed by the carpal bones and the ligament, pinching the median nerve that gives feeling to the hand. Symptoms of carpal tunnel syndrome include burning or painful tingling in a hand or shooting pains up an arm.

Carpal tunnel syndrome is not unique to computer operators. All types of workers who perform repetitive tasks are at risk for developing the condition — including garment workers, butchers, grocery checkers, electronics assembly workers, typists, musicians, packers, housekeepers, cooks, and carpenters.

Other illnesses associated with office automation, and computer usage in particular, that are reported more often by computer users than by non-users include:

— Neck, shoulder, and lower back pains.

— Headaches.

— Irritability.

— Difficulty sleeping.

— Deteriorated vision.

— Eye strain.

— Eye irritation.

— Red eyes.

— Blurred vision.

Some are concerned that the radiation emitted from computer monitors might also cause cataracts and birth defects. If you have employees who do the type of work that may make them prone to repetitive stress injuries or other automation-related illnesses, your best bet for protecting yourself — and your employees — is to take preventative measures.

Once you are aware of the office automation-related injuries and illnesses that your employees face, you can better prevent them.

Repetitive motion problems: If your jobs require repetitive motion, you can take some steps to minimise the risk to employees who do those jobs, including making sure that:

1. Work stations are ergonomically correct and have:
   — Adjustable components.
   — A foot rest.
   — A document holder.
   — A wrist rest.
2. Tools and work methods are designed properly.
3. Employees understand the risks of repetitive motion.
4. Productivity requirements are not resulting in inadequate rest breaks.

You can also consider rotating employees among different jobs to make sure that they don't have to perform the same motions all day long. Remember, the way that you arrange your computer equipment can go a long way toward avoiding computer pains.

Vision problems: Employees who must stare at computer monitors face special problems with their vision. Some ways to help minimise the risk of injury or illness include:

— Providing adjustable furniture and equipment, particularly at shared work stations.

— Reducing room lighting in the area to about half of what the customary office lighting is and providing desk lamps for other work.

— Encouraging computer operators to have a thorough eye examination every year.

— Allowing breaks or time for tasks that don't require close concentration.

— Shading windows to reduce glare on computer monitors.

— Providing desk equipment so that reference materials can be placed close to the computer monitor and at the same distance from the eyes.

— Educating employees on how prolonged staring at computer monitor screens may affect their eyes.

9.4.2. AIDS in the Workplace

AIDS has become a workplace issue because some employers and employees fear that this fatal disease can be transmitted in the workplace. Additionally, employees who have AIDS fear that they will lose their job, benefits, friends, and more. Employers should worry about the health and peace of mind of all employees. Keep in mind that you can't segregate or penalise individuals with AIDS, or you risk running afoul of civil rights laws or the Americans with Disabilities Act.

You may feel that you are caught between two opposing forces — employees who are demanding protection and your inability to react as employees want. Since AIDS has become a workplace issue, other medical conditions, such as Hepatitis B virus (HBV), have also raised workplace concerns.

SUGGESTED READINGS

Barty Phillips. (2000). *The Home Office Planner*. Chronicle Books.

Don Aslett. (1995). *The Office Clutter Cure: How to Get Out from Under It All*. John Caldwell Betterway Books.

Julie Morgenstern. (2004). *Making Work Work: New Strategies for Surviving and Thriving at the Office*. Fireside

_____________. (2004). *Organizing from the Inside Out: The Foolproof System For Organizing Your Home, Your Office and Your Life*. Owl Books.

Lisa Kanarek. (1998). *Organizing Your Home Office For Success: Expert Strategies That Can Work for You*. Blakely Press.

Neal Zimmerman. (1996). *Home Office Design: Everything You Need to Know About Planning, Organizing, and Furnishing Your Work Space*. Wiley.

Niall Barrett. (2002). *The Custom Home Office: Building a Complete Workspace*. Taunton.

Odette Pollar. (1999). *Organizing Your Work Space: A Guide to Personal Productivity*. Crisp Learning.

Ronni Eisenberg. (1999). *Organize Your Office! Simple Routines for Managing Your Workspace*. Hyperion.

Stephanie Winston. (2001). *The Organized Executive: A Program for Productivity—New Ways to Manage Time, Paper, People, and the Electronic Office*. Warner Business Books.

_____________. (2004). *Organized for Success: Top Executives and CEOs Reveal the Organizing Principles That Helped Them Reach the Top*. Crown Business.

More titles are available in

MANAGEMENT BOOKS

Improve your Marketing and Grow your Business **(New)**	150/-
What Customers Really Want **(New)**	150/-
Effective Presentation **(New)**	150/-
Right Decision Every Time **(New)**	150/-
Develop Your Decision Making Skills **(New)**	95/-
Develop Your Team Building Skills **(New)**	95/-
Develop Your Skills to Conduct Effective Meetings **(New)**	95/-
How to Export Import	95/-